**SPIRAL GUIDE**

LANZAROTE

**Publishing**

# Contents

## *the magazine* 5

## Finding Your Feet 39

## The North 49

## The Centre 75

Written and updated by Paul Murphy
Produced by Cambridge Publishing Management Ltd

Update managed by Bookwork Creative Associates Ltd

Published by AA Publishing, a trading name of AA Media Limited,
whose registered office is Fanum House, Basing View, Basingstoke,
Hampshire RG21 4EA. Registered number 06112600.

ISBN 978-0-7495-4742-4

The content of this book is believed to be accurate at the time of
printing. Due to its nature the content is likely to vary or change and
the publisher is not responsible for such change and accordingly is
not responsible for the consequences of any reliance by the reader on
information that has changed. Any rights that are given to consumers
under applicable law are not affected. Opinions expressed are for
guidance only and are those of the assessor based on their experience
at the time of review and may differ from the reader's opinions based
on their subsequent experience.

We have tried to ensure accuracy in this guide, but things do
change, so please let us know if you have any comments at
travelguides@theAA.com.

A CIP catalogue record for this book is available from the British
Library

© AA Media Limited 2002, 2005, 2008
Information verified and updated 2008
Reprinted March 2011.

Cover design and binding style by permission of AA Publishing
Colour separation by Leo Reprographics
Printed and bound in China by Leo Reprographics

Find out more about AA Publishing and the wide range of services
the AA provides by visiting our website at theAA.com/shop

A04682
Maps in this title produced from mapping © MAIRDUMONT / Falk
Verlag 2011

*the magazine*

# Fields of Fire

"Suddenly the earth opened up near Timanfaya…the lava flowed towards the north as rapidly as water but it soon thickened and slowed down, flowing as if it were honey… In an instant the mass of glowing lava reached out and destroyed the villages of Maretas and Santa Catalina in the valley. The darkness caused by the mass of ashes and smoke covering the sky and shutting out the sun caused the inhabitants of Yaiza to flee…"

*Diary of the Yaiza parish priest, Don Andrés Lorenzo Curbelo, 1 September, 1730.*

The Timanfaya eruptions lasted for another six years, the longest and largest recorded historical eruptions in the Canary Islands, with 26 volcanoes blowing their tops, or sides, at one time or another. It is said that the sounds of the explosions were so loud that they were heard in Tenerife, 250km (155 miles) away!

When the ground stopped shaking, about 200sq km (78 square miles) – one-third of the island, including many villages and hamlets plus the most fertile valleys and estates – was buried under the lava. It is estimated that the average depth of lava in

**Take a camel trip through the Timanfaya National Park…**

the area of today's national park is an incredible 4m (13 feet) – over twice the height of the average man. Ironically, the huge lava field, which was spewed from the volcanoes, also increased the island size by one-third.

Fortunately, Canarian volcanoes are what are known as the Hawaiian type, which are relatively slow to burn and give plenty of notice before erupting. The area was therefore evacuated and remarkably no one was killed or even injured. With their most fertile fields laid waste, many of the islanders were reduced to destitution and sought to flee Lanzarote. Some did, but the Spanish authorities, fearing that an empty island would be seized as a strategic maritime base by rival powers (including the English), prohibited

**...and take in the breadth of the volcanic landscape**

further evacuation under pain of death.

In 1824 three more volcanoes exploded just outside the boundary of the current national park. It is said that the heat was suffocating and sailors could hardly see the island because of the dense mist generated. Once again, there were no casualties and the damage, compared to the previous eruptions, was minimal, but it was still a terrifying experience:

"On September 29 the volcano burst through the lava deposit of 1730, and flaming torrents flowed down to the sea. A noise like loud thunder had continued unceasingly, and prevented the inhabitants from sleeping, even many miles away. It is now 18 October and there is no doubt a furnace under our feet…yesterday the volcano burst through a bed of lava in the centre of a great plain, sending up into the air a column of boiling water 150ft high."

*From letters written by Don Augustin Cabrera, a local inhabitant*

Since then there have been no more explosions, and the only current geothermal energy in the park has been harnessed as a visitor attraction (▶ 105).

## The volcanic landscape

There is a total of 125 volcanic cones on Lanzarote, and because of the island's arid climate this is the perfect place for seeing exactly what happened during the eruptions. In many other volcanic destinations in the world, such as Hawaii or Costa Rica, lush vegetation covers the traces, but here it is bare for all to see.

There are three main types of volcanic debris on Lanzarote. The biggest type is known as a bomb, which can range from the size of a grapefruit to a large boulder. Bombs are dense with a brittle overcoat, which is sometimes broken open to reveal the semi-precious green stone, olivine. Next in size comes pumice, *escoria* or slag – smaller, lightweight rock, honeycombed by hot gases. The smallest debris is *picón* or *lapilli*, the tiny light cinder particles put to good effect by Canarian farmers and wine growers.

The lava flow also divides into two main types,

**See the black sands of El Golfo**

classified by Hawaiian terms. When thick, slow-flowing lava cools and breaks up, the rocks are rough and jagged. This lava is called *aa* (pronounced "ah-ah") and forms the classic Canarian *malpaís* (badlands) landscape. Thinner, faster-flowing lava, which cools quickly and is consequently smoother in texture, is known as *pahoehoe* or *pahoe-pahoe*.

Another important feature is the volcanic tube, which is created by rivers of lava. The tube forms when the outer layer of the lava flow cools and solidifies, but the lava beneath the surface remains fluid and continues to flow. When the roof of a volcanic tube collapses it is known as a *jameo* ("ha-may-oh").

## Learning more about volcanoes

The best exhibition on the island's volcanic activity is the Casa de los Volcanes in the Jameos del Agua (► 59–61). The Interpretation Centre at Mancha Blanca (► 105) has a similar but less interesting exhibition, but a fascinating walk is led from here into the Termesana area of the park by rangers, free of charge. You must be 16 or older and book

in advance, tel: 928 840 839. By far the best way of learning about the island's vulcanology is to take the Canary Trekking tour. It is led by a well-informed former park ranger, who will happily answer your questions. At around 7km (4 miles) this is much longer than the Termesana tour and relatively expensive but will probably be one of the highlights of your holiday (tel: 609 537 684, www.canarytrekking. com). The tour ends at the sight of the 1824 explosions where you can look right down into the volcanic "chimneys" caused by the enormous boiling waterspouts.

Learn about the science of it all at the Mancha Blanca Visitors' Centre

# CÉSAR MANRIQUE

Wherever you go on Lanzarote you will come across the name César Manrique, or, if not the name, then his influence. From surreally landscaped visitor attractions to designer restaurant menus, from art galleries to street sculptures, from restored mansions to the island logo, it is impossible to escape the man. It is universally agreed that the set-piece attractions and art works that Manrique has bequeathed to the island are extraordinary in themselves, but the measure of his greatness is also in what is not on the island and the values that he has embedded into future generations of Lanzaroteños.

César Manrique was born in Arrecife in 1919. He studied at art college in Madrid and at the age of 23 staged his first exhibition in Arrecife with the aid of Pepin Ramírez, a family friend who would later become a vital ally.

Manrique's early artworks were conventional in style and subjects, with many works featuring the island and its islanders, but when Surrealism burst on the scene in the mid-1950s he became a torch carrier for the movement and opened Spain's first non-figurative art gallery. He rapidly made a name for himself, and in 1964 Nelson Rockefeller, who had bought some of his works, invited him to exhibit in the USA. Manrique flourished there and lived in New York for two years before the call of his beloved island beckoned him home. By now Pepin Ramírez was president of the Cabildo

*César Manrique's work can be seen all over the island*

island council and enthusiastically supported the ideas that his old friend had in store for Lanzarote.

Noting the effect that mass tourism and increasing commercialisation was exerting on developing holiday destinations (such as Gran Canaria and Tenerife), Manrique and Ramírez drew up a series of guidelines that are still implemented to this day. The most apparent were a ban on advertising hoardings, electricity pylons and high-rise buildings, and all new buildings had to conform to the native island style – whitewashed with doors and windows painted green or brown in the countryside and blue by the sea. Manrique's philosophy was that the island's traditional design had evolved over hundreds of years of experience on how best to adapt to the climate. An equilibrium and harmony had been achieved between man and nature and this is what he sought to preserve. Long before it was fashionable, or perhaps even considered, his aim was sustainable development.

"Man has had to become gradually integrated in the tiny nooks of nature to find the truth of life. All I want to do is be a part of nature, so that it may help me and I may help it."

Manrique had begun to conceive his magnificent seven visitor attractions (now known as the Centros de Arte, Cultura y Turismo) even while he was in New York, mailing his ideas for the first of these, the Jameos del Agua, to Ramírez. His works were to be "dreams that capture the sublime natural beauty of Lanzarote". Over the next decade he was to add the International Museum of

Look out for roadside mobiles designed by Manrique

Contemporary Art at the Castillo de San José (▶85); the Cueva de los Verdes (▶62); the Mirador del Río (▶65); the El Diablo restaurant, Timanfaya (▶103); the Casa Monumento al Campesino; and the Jardín de Cactus (▶63). He was also busy working on major projects elsewhere; the Lago Martiánez lido at Puerto de la Cruz in Tenerife; two *miradores* (belvederes) on the Canary Islands of El Hierro and La Gomera; and La Vaguada, a Madrid shopping centre.

"On Lanzarote we have worked with utter devotion, in close contact with geology, understanding its composition and its volcanic essence, achieving a miracle of a new aesthetic."

*Manrique, from the book In His Own Words by Fernando Gómez Aguilera.*

By 1988 Manrique's celebrity status meant that he could no longer work undisturbed by fans and well-wishers at his famous house at Taro de Tahiche (▶54–55) and he moved to Haría. His house continued to function as the Fundación César Manrique. He continued working full time into his 70s, but in 1992 he was tragically knocked over by a car and killed, just 50m (55 yards) away from Taro de Tahiche. He is buried in a simple grave at Haría.

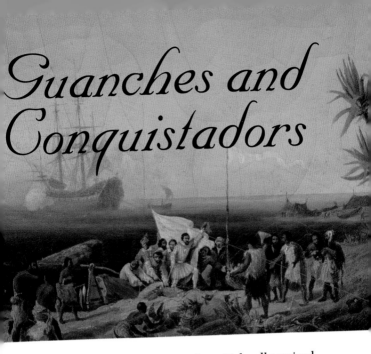

# Guanches and Conquistadors

When the Genoan sea captain Lancelotto Malocello arrived on Lanzarote in 1312, a curious sight awaited him. Here were a people only slightly removed from the Stone Age in appearance and technology. Its inhabitants knew the island as Tyteroygaka (or Titeroyugatra), meaning the red mountain, but to outsiders it thereafter became Lanzarote, the Hispanic version of Lancelotto.

Malocello did not stay and the precise purpose of this first European visit remains a mystery, but a century later the Norman baron Jean de Béthencourt arrived in the islands with two objectives in mind. His first was commercial, to discover from where the fabled "River of Gold" traffic was pouring out of the Sahara, and his second was to convert the natives, known as Guanches ("gwan-chez"), to Christianity.

De Béthencourt's priests recorded that they were a peaceful people with high moral standards: "go throughout the world and nowhere will you find a finer and better formed people…

Jean de Béthencourt came to the island in the 15th century

with great minds were they to receive instructions."

The chronicles continued: "it [Lanzarote] contains many villages and fair houses, and used to be well peopled, but the Spaniards and other corsairs of the sea have so frequently made captures that…when de Béthencourt arrived there were scarcely 300 inhabitants whom he conquered with much labour and great trials, and by the grace of God had them baptised.

The inhabitants are a fine race. The men go quite naked; except for a cloak over their shoulders, which reaches to their thighs, they are indifferent to other covering. The women are beautiful and modest. They wear long leather robes which reach down to the ground."

Other researchers added that their hair was long, the men wore plaited beards and that their clothes and shoes were made of goatskins.

German naturalist, geographer and Canarian expert, Alexander von Humboldt, concurred in an account of the islanders during his research in 1799.

"On the arrival of the Spaniards its [Lanzarote's] inhabitants were distinguished from the other Canarians by marks of greater civilisation. Their homes were built with free stone [without cement, lime or mortar] while the Guanche inhabitants of Tenerife dwelt…in caverns."

**German naturalist Alexander von Humboldt**

## An unfortunate turn of events

It seems that a violent

conquest was not on de Béthencourt's agenda but that events simply took their own course. On landing near the site of present-day Playa Blanca (►111) he met the island king, Guadarfía, and established a pact of friendship with him.

Shortly afterwards he made a reconnaissance trip to Fuerteventura, and, deciding that he would need reinforcements for this part of his mission, sailed back to Spain leaving his second-in-command, Gadifer de la Salle, in charge.

Unfortunately, while he (de la Salle) was away, on Isla de Lobos, some of his men absconded, taking a number of natives with them as slaves. The rest of the islanders were enraged by this and killed some of the remaining Europeans. When Gadifer returned he swore to avenge these deaths. Fierce fighting ensued and those islanders who were not killed were captured and taken into slavery. King Guadarfía surrendered voluntarily and was allowed to retain his lands along with a few of his most loyal men.

According to local lore, Guadarfía's daughter, the Princess Teguise, married Jean de Béthencourt's nephew and successor, Maciot de Béthencourt, thus appearing to tie up the story neatly. There was to be no happy ever after, however, as one of Maciot's first actions was to sell Lanzarote to the Portuguese. The islanders repelled the Portuguese force and Maciot was deposed.

Guanches, or early Canary islanders

## The early islanders

The Guanches were not in fact the original islanders. That honour belonged to African Berber migrants who came to the Canaries around 3000 BC. The Guanches, who did not arrive until the 1st or 2nd century BC, may have had links with these Berber peoples but their origins are unclear.

## Spain's gain

If the French court had backed Jean de Béthencourt's adventures, Canary Islanders today might be speaking French instead of Spanish. The French refused to finance him so the Norman knight took his proposal to Castile who accepted on condition that the conquered territories would belong to them.

# Food and Drink

Genuine Canarian cuisine is all about dishes that originated in the kitchens of the rural and fishing community, typified by hearty stews and simple barbecued fish. International may be prevalent in parts of Puerto del Carmen and Costa Teguise, but thankfully the majority of restaurants on the island still serve a mix of Spanish and Canarian food.

## Mojo and papas

The Canary Islands' most distinctive tastes are *mojo picón* and *mojo verde. Mojo picón*, (literally "piquant sauce") is made from chilli peppers, garlic, cumin, paprika and vinegar. It is always served cold and normally accompanies meat dishes and *papas arrugadas* ("wrinkly potatoes"). The latter is another Canarian staple – small new potatoes boiled in, and served with, a generous sprinkling of sea salt. They are nearly always delicious and rarely taste too salty. By contrast to the fiery red variety, *mojo verde* (green sauce) is a cool fresh blend, substituting coriander for chilli, and always accompanies fish.

## Island specials: meat and cheese

Goat is popular for its cheese and meat. *Queso de cabra* (goats' cheese) is a common starter, usually served with sliced tomatoes. It may also be fried in breadcrumbs and served with quince jam (*membrillo*), palm honey (*miel de palma*), or perhaps *mojo verde*. Look under "specialities" for kid (*cabrito*), which is either fried, baked or served in a stew (*compuesta*).

Some restaurants only serve goat or kid stew on Sunday at lunchtime and specify that it must be ordered ahead. Lamb is another Sunday special. Rabbit (*conejo*) is also popular, often served either in a special tomato-based stew (*al salmorejo*) or fried. Steaks are usually good quality – some restaurants display them uncooked in a refrigerated cabinet – and come from Argentina.

## Island fish and seafood

The cheapest fish on most restaurant menus is usually *sardines* (sardines) but it's usually worth paying a bit more for *cherne* (translated as both grouper and stone bass), *vieja* (parrotfish), *sama* (sea bream) or *gallo*, *mero* and *viuda*, local fish that have no satisfactory translation. Other popular fish and seafood items caught locally include *atún* (tuna), *pez espada* (swordfish), *merluza* (hake) and *lenguado* (sole).

Most of these are served simply barbecued or fried. More elaborate dishes include fish baked in salt (don't worry, the salt is removed before serving and, surprisingly, it won't taste too salty) and fish stew; generally either *zarzuela* (also known as *cazuela*), from mainland Spain, a rich tomato-based concoction with shellfish, or the typically Canarian *sancocho*, comprising salt fish (dried cod) and potatoes.

**Fresh fish features high on the menu and you can usually eat outside in the sun**

## Tasty tapas and starters

*Albóndigas* (meatballs)
*Calamares* (fried battered squid)
*Chorizos al vino tinto* (paprika sausage in red wine)
*Gambas* (prawns)
*Jamón serrano* (mountain cured ham). *Pata negra* is the best variety, and very expensive.
*Mejillones* (mussels)
*Pimientos* (peppers). These may be stuffed with a variety of fillings. *Pimientos de padrón* are the hot spicy variety. They are sometimes served smothered in melted cheese.
*Pulpo* (octopus)
*Tortilla* (potato omelette)

Ever popular is that sizzling Spanish starter *gambas al ajillo* (prawns in garlic and spicy tomato sauce or very hot olive oil) and paella, Spain's national dish, typically including mussels, prawns and often rabbit. Try *lapas* (limpets), which are similar to mussels – another common island dish – but meatier and with a slightly earthy taste.

Smoked salmon, although not indigenous, has been popularised by the smokehouse at Uga (► 116) and frequently appears on the menu at more upmarket restaurants. Less common, but equally delicious, is smoked tuna.

## Sweet things

In many local establishments the choice of *postres* (desserts) is restricted to *flan* (the ubiquitous Spanish crème caramel) or *helado* (ice cream). Keep an eye out for

**Visit one of the wineries and try some *malvasia seco***

the following: *frangollo,* which is made of *gofio* (▶ below) and dried fruit soaked in syrup; *bienmesabe* (ground almonds, egg yolks and sugar syrup blended to the consistency of honey), often served with ice cream or bananas; *leche asada* (literally "baked milk", a kind of lemony sponge milk pudding); *leche frita* ("fried milk"), also like crème caramel; and *gofio mousse* (▶ below).

## Vegetarian vicissitudes

Fish aside, it's hard to get a true vegetarian meal in a local restaurant. Even dishes like *potaje de berros* (watercress soup) or *garbanzos compuestos* (chickpea stew) include bacon or pork. The best bet is the newer style of restaurants, many of which make a point of offering interesting Spanish or locally inspired vegetarian dishes.

## Gofio – the staff of life

*Gofio,* flour made by grinding roasted barley, maize or wheat, has been the Canarian staple since Guanche times (▶ 13–15). It is typically eaten by islanders as porridge or a kind of polenta, or is used to thicken soups and stews. It also occasionally finds its way onto the tourist menu under *gofio escaldado*

(combined with fish stock), *helado de gofio* (*gofio* ice cream) or perhaps *mousse de gofio.*

## And to drink...

Even though the island's wines have a long and famous history, you will find that most table wine is from mainland Spain. The reason for this is cost (island wines are not produced in bulk) and misconceptions that all Lanzarote wines are sweet. However, a

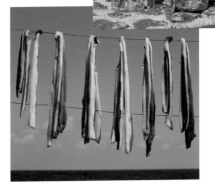

*malvasia seco* or even *semi-seco* (medium dry) is a good white table wine and there are island reds too. You can taste as many as you like at the island's *bodegas,* or wine bars (▶ 69 and 108).

**Fish hanging out to dry is an unusual sight**

## More Canarian specialities

*Potaje* or *puchero canarias* – a hearty meat and vegetable casserole that may be served with *gofio* dumplings.

*Rancho canario* – a stew of meat, potatoes, chickpeas, tomatoes and noodles.

*Ropa vieja* – literally "old clothes", a stew of meat, chickpeas and whatever vegetables the chef fancies throwing in.

# TRANSPORTS OF DELIGHT

## Take flight

There's only one way to look right down into the craters of Timanfaya, to float above the Caldera Blanca (the biggest complete crater in the archipelago), to peer in to the King of Spain's holiday home, or to see just why Arrecife was so named (after the offshore reefs that make it a natural harbour) – and that's from the air. You have two choices. The helicopter is smoother and, for nervous passengers, generally feels safer. Up to six people can ride along for 30 minutes (€176) or 50 minutes (€276). Lanza Air's single-prop four-seater Cessna is a real buzz too. It costs €250 for either two or three people and lasts one hour.

**Heli Tourservice**, Lanzarote airport, Arrecife, tel: 676 701 693. www.excursiononline.com
**Lanza Air**, tel: 928 590 533, www.lanzarote.com/lanzaair

## One hull or two?

You'll find the island's best selection of boats at Puerto Calero marina, just south of Puerto del Carmen. A day aboard the Catlanza (tel: 928 513 022, 609 667 246, www.catlanza.com), a 23m (75-foot) luxury catamaran, is highly recommended. The Anglo-Irish-Canarian crew are great fun and will happily take you to the Papagayo beaches (▶ 109). They offer jet-ski rides and, if you are lucky, you may even get to snorkel with dolphins. If it's a more conventional sailing trip you're after, simply ask around at the port – McSorley's is the best place to start, and you'll soon find someone willing to take you out. It's a great opportunity to learn more about sailing with a friendly, experienced crew. If there's a group of you, consider a day charter.

## Avoiding the hump

There's only one animal that is designed to cope with the island climate and the surface

**(Right)** There are many boat-hire and sailing options

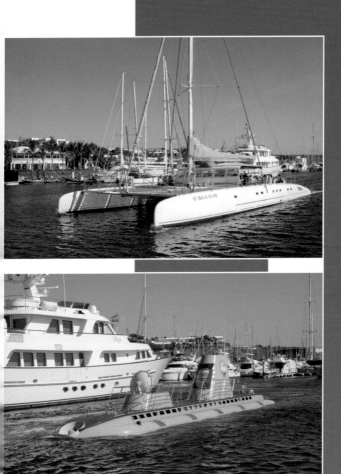

of Lanzarote's Fire Mountains and that is the camel, or dromedary in this case. The yoke-like seat that accommodates passengers, one slung on either side like so much cargo, is called *la silla inglesa* (the English chair), as it was specially designed for saddle-sore tourists, most of whom were English, in the 19th century. You're not exactly going to look like Lawrence of Arabia but neither will you fall off. And how many opportunities in your life are you going to get to take a camel up a volcano? (▶6–9).

Try riding
a camel or
exploring on
a bicycle

## Dive, Dive, Dive!

With a perfect sky of blue
and a clear sea of green, all
you need is a yellow
submarine, which is exactly
what's on offer at Submarine
Safaris at Puerto Calero.
SubFun3, as she is known,
is 18.5m (60 feet) long, 4m
(13 feet) wide and weighs
106 tons. She can descend to
60m (200 feet) and
accommodates up to 48
passengers and crew with 22
large portholes, or view ports.
Each view port has its own
TV monitor giving alternative
viewing angles, along with a
digital display panel giving
continuous information about
the submarine. The dive lasts
around an hour, during
which a tour guide points out
the various sea life – an
accompanying diver with
food ensures a good selection
of local fish drop by – and a
recent wreck (tel: 928
512898, or 928 512906;
www.submarinesafaris.com).

## On yer bike

The toughest test of all is one
only for experienced cyclists,
but once you've seen the
athletes of Club La Santa
tearing up Lanzarote's roads
in their multicoloured skin-
tight suits you'll want to do it
too. There's just something
so cool about the contrast
between the monochrome
primeval landscape and
polychromatic 21st-century
hi-tech cyclists. The best
place to hire from is
Ciclomania in Arrecife
(► 96).

# Living off the Land

## "Strange Fruits and Commodities"

Lanzarote receives less rainfall than some parts of the Sahara, its most fertile fields were destroyed in the volcanic eruptions of the 1730s and its age-old commodities of salt and cochineal have been overtaken by new technologies. Yet still the *campesinos* (peasants) work the land, producing minor miracles daily.

### Cochineal, carmine and Campari

In 1583 the very first book about the Canary Islands was written by Thomas Nichols. It was titled *A Pleasant Description of the Fortunate Islands Called The Islands of Canaria with their Strange Fruits and Commodities* and mentioned orchil (a much sought-after plant from which dye is extracted), which had been traded on the island as far back as the time of the Conquest. The purplish orchil dye was to be superseded by another red dye, called carmine, extracted from the cochineal beetle. This tiny insect feeds on a special strain of cactus, specifically imported from Mexico in the mid-19th century where they have been producing carmine going back to pre-Columbian times. On the leaf the beetles look like a grey mould, but when crushed emit a gory blood-red dye. During the

19th century, carmine (or "carmine-cochineal") was once exported in great quantities to the European textile industry. For a time it was the mainstay of the island's economy, but the market collapsed with the introduction of cheaper artificial dyes towards the end of the century. Carmine was also used as a colouring agent in foods such as pork sausages, pies, shrimps, sweets, jams and bright red maraschino cherries. It went into cosmetics (lipstick and rouge) and drinks too. Recently the carmine market has made something of a comeback due to carcinogenic health scares about the use of artificial dyes, particularly in the food and drink industry. Major brand-name products it appears in today include Campari and Tropicana Ruby Red grapefruit juice.

The island's cochineal centre is around Guatiza (►63).

**Horseshoe-shaped shelters protect the vines from the wind**

## Salt sellers

Salt has been recovered from the sea for centuries on the island and has been in demand by the Arrecife fishing fleet since the 1500s. Conveniently, just as carmine demand declined, so salt boomed worldwide. The island's saltpans flourished – at Salinas de Janubio (►110), beneath the Mirador del Río; at Puerto Naos, Arrecife and elsewhere around the island – but with the advent of refrigeration, the industry went into decline and today the Salinas de Janubio is the sole survivor.

## Crops from the ashes

Although the cataclysmic eruptions of 1730–36 (►6)

wiped out the best arable lands, shortly afterwards the farmers noticed, much to their surprise, that green shoots were emerging from beneath the *picón* (lava granules). Because of its porous nature, this stone was retaining what little moisture there was from the dew and drip-feeding it down to the plants' roots, deep in the soil, which could be covered by a layer of *picón* several metres deep. The only problem was to protect the plants from the wind. Using the plentiful supply of larger volcanic stones that lay all

around them, the islanders set to building horseshoe-shaped shelters of drystone walls, about a metre high, around each plant. These are known as *zocos* and are found in many places on the island, most famously in the wine-growing area of La Geria (► 107–108).

It is not just vines that grow in the black volcanic soil. Keep your eyes open while travelling around Femés, Los Valles and Haría, in particular, and you will see old men and women working in their black lava fields, planting and harvesting crops such as potatoes, onions, squash, water melon and so on – all by hand, just as they have done for centuries.

**Farming settlements are dotted across the landscape of Guinate**

**Harvesting both sea (left) and land (top)**

# THIS SPORTING LIFE

Mention Lanzarote and sport in the same breath and the response from most people will be "Club La Santa". But there is more to sport on the island than just this famous complex.

## Club La Santa

Club La Santa was conceived as a sporting centre in 1983 and is one of the largest complexes of its kind in Europe (www.clublasanta. com). Its facilities are only open to residents but it does organise two major events each year, which are open to the public. The Lanzarote Marathon, run in November or December, is both a fun run and a serious event, with a quarter-marathon, a half-marathon, a "mini-marathon" for children and the main 42.2km (26-mile) event which attracts club runners from all over Europe. There are around 1,000 participants in all, www.lanzarotemarathon.com

The event of the year is the Ironman Triathlon. It began in

For listings of all sports operators see the "Where to be Entertained" section under the relevant areas.

1992 and now attracts around 1,200 serious athletes each year. You have to be dedicated to put yourself through 3.8km (2.3 miles) of swimming, 180km (112 miles) of cycling, then for good measure run a full marathon – consecutively, with no break. Despite the macho name, women also compete. The event centres on Puerto del Carmen and takes place in May; see www.ironmanlanzarote.com.

Ironman involves the collaboration of around 2,000 island volunteers and, for a few days at least, generates

enormous interest around the island and beyond, with Spanish and international television crews present.

## Windsurfing

The Canary Islands have always benefited (and suffered) from heavy swells and strong winds, and the presence of acceleration zones makes Lanzarote one of the best places in Europe for experienced windsurfers. Acceleration zones occur where the wind is funnelled between mountains or small islands and can triple the wind's strength.

In summer the winds blow hard for at least 25 days per month, but they drop in winter, and with sheltered bays and plenty of expert advice Lanzarote is an excellent place for beginners and novices too. The prime location is Costa Teguise, which has been hosting Windsurf World Cup competitions each July for over a decade.

## Surfing and kiteboarding

The long, windswept beach of Famara is where many surfers get their kicks on Lanzarote, particularly during the winter months (October to March) when there is less wind and the waves are bigger. Isla la Graciosa is another surfers' destination.

There is also the opportunity to learn the exciting new sport of kiteboarding at Famara.

**Lanzarote is famous for its water sports**

## Big-game fishing

Puerto Calero is the best place for fishing charters. Boats regularly return with trophies, or at least photos (anglers are encouraged to tag and release) of tuna, dorado, amberjack, mahi-mahi, wahoo and marlin. World-record weight fishes have been caught from here and the Puerto Calero Fishing Tournament, held each September, sees around 50 boats in pursuit of the sport fisherman's ultimate quarry, the feisty blue marlin, which weigh in at more than 200kg (440lb).

Described as a cross between windsurfing, wakeboarding and paragliding, kitesurfers control a wing of lightweight fabric which pulls them across the water at speeds up to 70kph (43mph). The experts can fly up to 15m (50 feet) high in the air, performing all manner of gymnastics before coming down again some 70m (77 yards) from where they first took off. You don't have to be a surfer to start kitesurfing, though of course it helps. It's more important at the outset that you can handle a stunt kite properly and understand the nature of the wind. You don't need a great deal of strength, as the harness will take the strain off your arms.

## Golf

Golf Costa Teguise, just to the north of the resort, is the only 18-hole course on the island at present, though there are two more under construction. It is a picturesque 18-hole course set among lava-stone cacti and over 3,000 palms at the foot of a volcano with views to the sea. No handicap certificate is necessary. There is a driving range, pitch and putt greens and equipment rental (tel: 928 590 512, www.lanzarote-golf.com).

**People come here for the sea, but also for golf**

For more on windsurfing, surfing and kiteboarding, including full holiday packages, go to www.surflanzarote.com

# CARNAVAL AND FIESTA

**The islanders, like most good Spaniards, really let their hair down at Carnival time, but attending other fiestas can be equally rewarding.**

Carnaval (as it is spelled locally) is at its biggest and best in Arrecife, Puerto del Carmen and Teguise, though it is celebrated all over the island. The dates vary from year to year but it all starts around nine weeks before Easter (usually February or early March) with the *Verbena de la Sábana* (Sheet Party) where participants dress in a sheet and little else. After this the Carnival Queen and the Children's Queen are elected. The climax of festivities is the Friday before Shrove Tuesday

when the Carnival Drag Queen is chosen (a feature of Carnaval is that men always dress as women) and the grand parade of dozens of colourful floats takes place the following day. Street parties and processions shimmy and shake to the insistent beat of salsa, lubricated by an inexhaustible supply of *cuba libra* (rum and cola) served from street kiosks.

In Teguise the stars of the show are the scary-looking Diabletes ("Little Devils")

From carnival queen to drag queen, fancy dress is a must

who wear a bull mask complete with tongue and horns and white muslin trousers and jacket, painted with red and black diamonds and covered with bells. A shepherd's pouch made of kid attached to a stick by a cord is brandished at the children. In Arrecife the Parranda de los Buches is a bizarre centuries-old tradition featuring masked men in traditional costumes singing, dancing and hitting spectators with a *buche* (fish stomach or bladder) that has been inflated and put on a stick (*parranda* simply means spree or binge)! And if you think that is odd, wait until you see the strangest ceremony of all, *El Entierro de la Sardina* (The Burial of the Sardine), which symbolises the end of Carnaval and the beginning of Lent. On Ash Wednesday, a huge papier-mâché sardine is carried in mock funeral procession through the streets accompanied by the bizarre sight and sound of black-clad "mourners" wailing and crying. When it arrives at its appointed place at the harbour, fireworks inside the sardine are lit and it is literally blown to pieces.

## Fiesta!

The centrepiece of most fiestas is a procession with parishioners carrying an effigy of the saint or the Virgin shoulder-high through the streets, accompanied by troupes of local musicians in traditional dress. The more important fiestas will also have floats, street food and stalls, and fireworks. The most colourful are:

**Cabalgata de Los Reyes Magos** (Three Kings /Three Wise Men Parade) on 5–6 January. For the Spanish this is the equivalent of Christmas Eve. It is the day before they exchange presents and have a traditional dinner. The celebrations at Teguise are very colourful.

**Corpus Christi** in June (exact date varies, contact the tourist office in Arrecife, tel: 928 811 762). Celebrations are held all over the island but the finest sights are in Arrecife and in Teguise, where

**Watch out if you attend the Parranda de lo Buches**

beautiful flower-patterned carpets of coloured salt are created around the main church. Elsewhere in Spain real flowers are used, but with more salt than flowers on the island the locals have used their ingenuity and creativity. Arrecife is also the centre of a month of festivities throughout August.

**San Juan**, the night of 23–24 June. Although this is a fiesta for St John, it is part of an older (pagan) tradition – bonfires are lit all over the island to usher in summer. Haría is a good place to celebrate.

**Nuestra Señora del Carmen**, the second fortnight of July. This pays homage to the patron saint of fishermen with colourful boat processions carrying a statue of the Virgin at Puerto del Carmen, Playa Blanca and Caleta del Sebo (on La Graciosa). Teguise celebrates with a Folk Festival including Canarian wrestling, street parties, processions and artisan fairs.

**Nuestra Señora de los Dolores**, mid-September. A traditional pilgrimage (*romería*) is led to the parish church in Mancha Blanca to give thanks for salvation from the eruptions of 1824 (▶8). This is followed by a folklore festival, with representatives from the other islands, and a craft fair.

Traditional folk dancing takes place throughout the year

## Tips

If you know you will be in Lanzarote during Carnival time, be prepared to party and bring along some fancy dress – anything will do, the more colourful and more outlandish the better.

See www.lanzarote.com/carnaval-en.html for dates.

# ISLAND OF THE IMAGINATION

On a desert island where flames frequently belch from the earth and the locals did not emerge from the Stone Age until the 15th century, it takes little imagination to conjure up strange goings-on.

On screen, Lanzarote's volcanic landscape has doubled for faraway planets and prehistoric Earth on many occasions, with the most popular locations being Timanfaya and El Golfo. Most famous of all is the 1966 Hammer Hollywood schlock classic *One Million Years BC*. It introduced the young Raquel Welch, in an animal-skin bikini. Her performance gained her sex-symbol status and her image on the film's posters became iconic. The film was nonsense of the highest order with cavemen fighting dinosaurs. Film fans note – the Timanfaya ranger-guided walk (▶ 103) may even take you into Raquel's cave! Things went from hammy to plain bad in the next Hammer dino-fest, *When Dinosaurs Ruled the Earth* (1971). This was another Hammer Films Production, with the female interest this time being a former Playboy Playmate of the Year. *Journey to the Centre of the Earth* (1976) was little better with the bizarre sight of Kenneth More, a British matinee idol of the 1950s and early 1960s, playing second fiddle to brawling dinosaurs and men in ape suits.

Lanzarote has starred on the small screen too. In 1984 four *Doctor Who* TV episodes (Planet Of Fire) saw Lanzarote doubling as the planet Sarn, with Peter Davison as the Doctor. He remembers it well: "My favourite memory is filming my second to last *Dr Who* story on a

**Many films have been shot here, including *Enemy Mine*...**

beach in sunny Lanzarote. Unfortunately, it turned out to be reserved for nudists. By 10am it was crowded with naked Germans, who insisted on walking past the TARDIS."

In 1985 Wolfgang Petersen, famous for *Troy*, *The Perfect Storm*, *Air Force One*, *In the Line of Fire*, *Shattered* and the TV classic *Das Boot*, filmed *Enemy Mine* here. The basic story line is that a soldier from Earth crash-lands on an alien world and encounters an enemy species with whom he has to cooperate to survive. It's not as bad as it sounds!

### And one they haven't filmed (… yet)

The longest-running Canarian myth, and one that should be taken with a barrowful of Lanzarote's finest salt, is that Lanzarote, along with the Azores, Madeira and Cape Verde, is one of the remaining uppermost peaks of the semi-divine kingdom of Atlantis – destroyed by Zeus as a punishment for its decadence. It is said that the Guanches were the descendants from the last survivors of the sunken civilisation, and in accordance with Atlantis architecture – whatever that may have looked like – they built long, conic pillar-like monuments in red, black and white stone. A monument of this type is claimed to be one found at the archaeological site at Zonzamas – but no one has carbon-dated it to put it to the test.

…but the most famous of all is *One Million Years BC* starring Raquel Welch

# BESTS, IFS & MOSTS

## Best coach tours

○ Ruta de los Volcanes in the Timanfaya National Park (► 105). The only way to see the best of the park. (Don't take any other island coach tours, but hire a car instead.)

## Best walking tours

○ The Canary Trekking guided walk in Timanfaya (► 9) and the park ranger-guided Termesana walk in Timanfaya (► 9). The former is better, but the latter is free!

## Best island views

○ Mirador del Río (► 65): vertiginous views of Isla la Graciosa.
○ Peñas del Chache (► 64 and 144): looking down onto Famara.
○ Castillo de Santa Bárbara (► 57): looking down onto Teguise and across the island.
○ From a helicopter or light airplane tour (► 20): the reefs of Arrecife and Timanfaya National Park.

## Best crash course on vulcanology

○ Casa de los Volcanes at Jameos del Agua (► 59–62) or Canary Trekking's guided walk in Timanfaya.

## Best optical illusion

○ At the end of the Cueva de los Verdes tour (► 62) – we can't tell you more, as it would spoil the surprise!

## Best food with a view

○ Jardín de Cactus (► 63): staring out over the world's most creative cactus garden.
○ The "balcony" restaurants at Puerto del Carmen's old

Take in the views of the landscape, sea and local culture

- Bodega restaurant/wine bar in Puerto del Carmen (►88): the real deal.
- Bodega Uga in Uga. There's no menu or price list on view. The intimate setting, in a gorgeously restored old farmhouse, is perfect for a romantic *tête-à-tête* and the food is usually not far behind, but you have little idea what the bill is going to be and it is invariably expensive. Tel: 928 830 147.

## Best beaches
- Playas de Papagayo (►109): picture-book golden sands.
- Caletón Blanco (►65): great for children but often overlooked.

## Best place if you're 18–25
- "The Strip" by night, Puerto del Carmen (►81).

## If you only see one
- César Manrique attraction, make it the Jameos del Agua: Rita Hayworth called it "the Eighth Wonder of the World".

## If you only see one
- Museum, make it the Museo Etnográfico Tanit (►86).

## Most controversial building
- Gran Hotel, Arrecife (►92). Check it out yourself from

port: look down on the port and out to sea.
- Altamar, Gran Hotel, Arrecife (►90): dining in a glass box, 17 storeys above the capital.

## "Most beautiful nightclub in the world"
- Jameos del Agua (►59–61) – according to César Manrique. His other nightspot creation, LagOmar (►67 and 68), is pretty special too.

## Best wine producers
- Bodega La Geria in La Geria (►108): book a tour of this venerable vineyard.
- Bodega El Grifo (►86): good little museum and an attractive tasting area.

## Best bodegas (wine bars)
- Bodega El Chupadero (►108): very stylish and cosy.

**Take the heat out of the day with a cool drink at a waterfront café**

the bar or restaurant on the 17th floor.

## Most pleasant surprise/best makeover

- Arrecife town centre for its new promenade and general restoration programme – no longer "crushed by cruel concrete"!

## Most atmospheric/beautiful town

- Teguise. See it on Sunday when the crowds bring it to life, but return at least once more to really explore its historic streets in peace and quiet.

## Best al-fresco dining

- Patio del Vino, Teguise (► 69): in the flower-filled garden of a 15th-century palace.
- Puerto Calero: on the waterside, gazing longingly at the yachts.

## Best food in beautiful surroundings

- La Tegala, Mácher (► 89).
- LagOmar, Nazaret (► 68).

- La Era, Yaiza (► 112).

## Best place to get away from it all

- Spend the night on Isla Graciosa (► 66–67).

## Best place to get fit/spot sporting personalities

- Club La Santa (► 26).

## Best water sports locations

- Diving: Puerto del Carmen.
- Windsurfing: Costa Teguise.
- Surfing: Famara.

## Best shopping

- Teguise, but not at the market!

## Most unusual holiday home

- Spend your holiday in a converted water cistern at Casa El Aljibe in Los Valles (► 71).

## Most amazing house

- César Manrique's House at Taro de Tahiche (► 54): who else could make a designer home from five "worthless" holes in the ground!

## Best day on the water

- Catlanza catamaran (► 20).
- McSorley's Bar regatta, if you can bag a place on a yacht (► 89–90).

## Best place for an alternative holiday

- Tomaren Centre of Holistic Holidays (► 93).

## Most inappropriate quote

- "Lanzagrotty" – *Monty Python*.

## Best avoided

- Time-share touts, anywhere advertising "Real British…".

# FAMILY LANZAROTE

There aren't many activities off the beach for families with children in Lanzarote. You'll have to choose carefully if you're on a budget, and although adults may gasp at Timanfaya and La Geria, remember most children just don't "do" scenery!

## Making a splash

With just one white-knuckle waterslide, AquaPark is more suited to younger children than thrill-seeking teens. The other slides and rides are fun but tame. There are swimming pools, a bouncy castle, boats, trampolines and a small play area.
Avenida de Teguise, Teguise.
Tel: 928 592 128.
Daily 10–6.
Very expensive (€21 adults and €15 children aged 2–12 years).

## Parque Natural de Recreo Las Pardelas

This is the friendliest attraction on the island. The owners, Alison and Carlos, have a wonderful enthusiasm for all things natural on Lanzarote and share it personally with visitors to their charming small farm. You'll be given vegetables, salads and bread to feed the animals, there's a small adventure playground and donkey rides, and children can try their hand at pottery and other handicrafts. Meanwhile, Mum and Dad can relax with a glass of local wine and tapas.
Carretera Orzola-Ye 1km.
Tel: 928 842 545.

The Wild West Rancho Texas (top); resident at Guinate Tropical Park (left)

Daily 10–6 (open Jul, Aug, Sep until 7).
Adults €3, children aged 2–15 years €2.40.

## Rancho Texas

Younger children may get a kick out of this Wild West-themed zoo park. It has all the usual ingredients: birds, small animals, parrot shows, birds of prey shows and crocodile shows. Free pick-up from Puerto del Carmen and Costa Teguise daily, pick-up from Playa Blanca (small charge).
Calle Noruega,
Puerto del Carmen.
Tel: 928 841 286.
www.ranchotexaslanzarote.com
Daily 9:30–5:30.
Adults €14, children aged 2–12 years €9.

## A life on the ocean wave

Children can get bored on boat excursions, but the *Marea Errota* (► 116) does its best to keep their interest with pirate games. There are numerous glass-bottom boats but there is often not that much to see in the water. A trip on a real submarine is a better bet, albeit more expensive, with guaranteed sightings of wrecks and fish (► 96).

## Guinate Tropical Park

Attractively laid out among waterfalls, lakes and gardens, this park is host to over 1,300 exotic birds and small animals. The stars are the spectacular hornbills and the magnificently coloured parrots and *turacos*. However, a rather tired parrot show and a small playground hardly justify the admission price.
Guinate. Tel: 928 835 500, www.guinatepark.com.
Daily 10–5.
Adults €14, children aged 4–13 years €5.

## Water babies

Lanzarote is a good place for older children to take their first water sports lessons. Both windsurfing tuition and diving begins at ten years old. Body-boarding, or boogie boarding as it is also known, is the first step towards learning to surf, and kids can start this as soon as they are confident in the water. Shops all over the island sell bodyboards.

Cute animals and seaside fun

## Manrique for kids

Jameos del Agua and Cueva de los Verdes (► 59–62) are the two best Manrique bets to keep youngsters happy. Spotting the tiny albino crabs, the hands-on stations in the Casa de los Volcanes, and being a troglodyte should keep them happy!

# Finding Your Feet

# First Two Hours

### Arriving at Lanzarote Airport

- The Aeropuerto de Lanzarote, sometimes referred to as Guacimeta, is 6km (4 miles) south of Arrecife and 6km north (4 miles) of Puerto del Carmen on the east coast.
- The major car hire companies have desks in the arrivals hall. There are currency exchange facilities, a café and basic shops, including a bookshop where you can buy island maps.

### Getting to your resort from the airport

- The quickest but most expensive option is to take a taxi from outside the airport building. For a list of fares see www.spanish-airport-guide.com and navigate to Lanzarote. Sample fares include Puerto del Carmen €11 and Playa Blanca €31. Alternatively, go to the airport information desk on the upper floor and pick up the *Aeropuerto de Lanzarote Horarios y Servicios* guide. Under the heading TAXI it lists approximate rates to the resorts.
- The official rate per km is €0.45 by day or €0.55 by night, with a €1.65 supplement for airport pick-up. Taxi office tel: 928 522 211.
- Buses from the airport go only to Arrecife where you will have to catch another bus to your destination. Look for airport bus 22 which runs Mon–Fri 6:50am–10:45pm, or bus 23 which runs Sat 8:50am–10:15pm. For full timetable see www.arrecifebus.com. The fare from the airport to Arrecife is €0.90.

### Car hire at the airport

- The major car hire companies have offices at the airport.
- Car hire is widely available in the main resorts, so unless you are staying somewhere remote you have the option of travelling to your accommodation by bus or taxi then hiring a car when you get there (➤ 42 for more on car hire).
- Follow the one-way signs out of the airport towards Yaiza and Arrecife. When you arrive at a traffic island graced by a splendid César Manrique wind mobile it is decision time. Head towards Yaiza for Puerto del Carmen, Playa Blanca and all destinations to the south; head towards Arrecife for Costa Teguise and all destinations to the north.

### Arriving/departing from other islands
**Non-tourist services**

- Binter Canarias (tel: 902 391 392, www.binternet.com) offers daily flights to Lanzarote from the other Canary Islands.
- Trasmediterránea (tel: 902 454 645, www.trasmediterranea.es) and Naviera Armas (tel: 902 456 500, www.navieraarmas.com) operate a service from Playa Blanca to Corralejo and from Arrecife to the islands of Gran Canaria, Tenerife, La Palma and El Hierro.

**Tourist services**

- Passengers from Fuerteventura (Corralejo) may arrive at either Playa Blanca or Puerto del Carmen. Fred Olsen (tel: 902 100 107, www.fredolsen.es) and Naviera Armas (tel: 902 456 500, www.navieraarmas.com) run a daily service to Playa Blanca every two hours from around 7am to around 8pm. The Princesa Ico company operates a service between Corralejo and Puerto del Carmen; for more details (➤ 118).

## Tourist information offices

■ Most tourist office staff speak English and German and can issue maps and information in English and German, www.turismolanzarote.com

**Airport**
Arrivals Hall. Open: daily for flights, tel: 928 820 704.
For airport information tel: 928 846 001.

**Arrecife**
Bandstand, Calle Blas Cabrera Felipe s/n,
tel: 928 811 762. Mon–Fri 8–3 (8–2 in summer).

**Costa Teguise**
CC Los Charcos, Local 11–13, Avenida Islas Canarias,
tel: 928 827 130. Mon–Fri 9:30–1.

**Playa Blanca**
Calle El Varedero s/n,
tel: 928 519 018.
Mon–Fri 8–2; Jul, Aug, Sep Mon–Fri 9–2.

**Puerto del Carmen**
Avenida de las Playas,
tel: 928 513 351.
Mon–Fri 10–5, Sat 10–1; Jul, Aug, Sep Mon–Fri 10–4.

**Teguise**
Spinola Place, Plaza de la Constitución,
tel: 928 845 398.
Sun–Thu 10–5

# Getting Around

## Buses

■ Island buses (called *guaguas*, "gwa-gwas", in the Canarian dialect) are modern and comfortable. However, the service between resorts and places of interest is often infrequent. Tickets are bought on board. Pick up a timetable from the nearest bus station or tourist office or click on www.lanzarote.com/guaguas/guaguas-in.html

**Useful services**

■ Bus no 1: Arrecife-Costa Tequise.
■ Bus no 2: Arrecife–Puerto del Carmen, which runs along the Avenida de las Playas every 20–30 minutes.
■ Bus no 6: Playa Blanca–Arrecife, though this is an infrequent service with a long wait between buses.
■ For bus information, tel: 928 811 522.
■ There is also a free private bus service that runs to and from the Biosfera Plaza Shopping Centre in Puerto del Carmen to Arrecife and Playa Blanca.

## Taxis

■ Taxis are usually white and have a green light on the top which is illuminated when they are available for hire.
■ For local journeys fares are metered (€0.45–€0.55 per km). If travelling across municipal boundaries the meter does not apply and you must agree a fare in advance.
■ You can get a list of taxi fares from Arrecife from the airport tourist office (➤ above).
■ You can usually hail a taxi on the street. The resorts and Arrecife have taxi ranks, but at night book through your hotel.
■ Taxi telephone number: 928 522 211.

## Driving

- If you want to explore you need to hire a car.
- Away from Arrecife and the main resorts there is not much traffic, roads are well surfaced and signposting is generally adequate.
- *Miradores* (lookout points) are usually provided in the mountains at particularly scenic spots so that you can pull over safely to enjoy the view.

## Car hire

- The major international car hire companies have offices at the airport, but local companies usually offer the best deals.
- To hire a car you will need your passport, driving licence and credit card. Keep these papers on you at all times, along with the car hire documents.
- If you intend driving off road, hire a 4WD/jeep vehicle that the car hire company recommends for this purpose. These are available from all the main operators, but book as far in advance as possible as they have limited numbers. If you have an accident or damage the underside of any other vehicle while driving off road your insurance will not cover this.
- It's usually worth paying that bit extra for air-conditioning.

## Driving essentials

- Drive on the right-hand side of the road.
- Seat belts are compulsory for the driver and all passengers.
- The legal alcohol limit is 80mg alcohol per 100ml blood.
- Speed limits are 90kph (56mph) on the open road and 40kph (25mph) in urban areas unless otherwise indicated.
- Petrol is much cheaper than in northern Europe and on mainland Spain. Petrol stations are few and far between in the mountains, so keep your tank topped up. Most, but not all, accept credit cards.
- Theft from cars is not a problem; nonetheless, lock valuable items in the boot.
- Blue lines indicate pay and display metered parking areas; yellow lines mean no parking.

## Maps

- Go to the tourist information office downstairs at the airport and pick up the excellent free Cabrera Medina Rent a Car road map.

## Admission charges

- The cost of admission for museums and places of interest mentioned in the text is indicated by the following categories:
  Inexpensive = under €3   Moderate = €3–6   Expensive = €6–9
  Very Expensive = €10+

# Accommodation

Tour operators book the majority of hotels and apartments, so independent travellers may experience some difficulty in finding places to stay.

Timeshare touts can be a nuisance in Puerto del Carmen and Costa Teguise. Be wary of anyone stopping you in the street or offering free excursions or prizes. Hard-sell tactics will follow this in order to get your signature on a property deal. The golden rule is sign nothing without consulting your lawyer.

## Hotels

- All hotels are officially graded from 1 to 5 stars, with most establishments rated as 3 stars or higher. In this category all bedrooms have a private bathroom.
- The hotels and apartments within this book have been selected because of their quality, special character or for being good value within their class or price range.
- Accommodation is generally more expensive in the winter, though December and January (excluding Christmas festivities) are quiet as the weather is often poor. There is a peak in late July and August when many Spanish families, as well as northern Europeans, are on holiday.
- The larger hotels encourage half board and some make it a condition. Others go the whole way, making it only a few euros more for full board or even all-inclusive.
- The newest hotels are in the south, at Playa Blanca.

## Apartments

- Apartments are graded from 1 to 3 keys, and even the simplest will have a bedroom, bathroom, lounge, kitchenette and balcony. Bed linen, bath towels and maid service are usually included in the price; equipment such as TVs, kettles and toasters can usually be hired for an extra charge. Aparthotels are large apartment blocks with all the facilities of a hotel, such as a swimming pool, restaurant and evening entertainment.
- The majority of self-catering accommodation is pre-booked by package tourists, but if you ask around in a resort you can usually find an apartment to let.

## Casas rurales

- Lanzarote's country hotels and apartments are some of the nicest in the Canaries, incorporating flair, style, often a touch of luxury and most mod cons (air conditioning is the only exception) into beautiful old whitewashed properties. Many holiday homes have been converted from traditional 19th-century farmhouses.
- For the best selection of rural properties try the following sites: www.lanzarote.com/reservas/turismorural-en.html www.islaviva.com
- The most common location for *Hoteles rurales* (rural hotels) is the centre of the island, particularly around San Bartolomé.

## Camping

- Lanzarote has three campsites, though facilities are basic and you need your own tent. Campsites open from June to September only. Camping de Papagayo is located at Playa de Puerto Muelas at the far end of the Papagayo beaches east of Playa Blanca (tel: 928 173 724).
- There is a campsite, El Salao, on La Graciosa but you will have to make arrangements at the town hall in Teguise before you go (tel: 928 845 985).
- Camping is also permitted in Famara at Camping de San Juan, but there are no facilities; contact Teguise town hall first, tel: 928 845 985.

## Prices

- The symbols refer to the average cost of a double room or one-bedroom apartment in high season. In the case of larger hotels these are published "rack rates" and can usually be negotiated down. € under €60   €€ €60–90   €€€ €91–120   €€€€ over €120

# Food and Drink

Most restaurants in Lanzarote offer Canarian cuisine (➤ 16–19) together with steaks, seafood dishes and traditional Spanish favourites. Fresh fish is available all over the island.

## What and where to eat

■ Resorts such as Puerto del Carmen, Costa Teguise and Playa Blanca have a full range of restaurants offering English breakfasts, hamburgers, pizzas, Wiener schnitzel and other reminders of home to their international clients.

■ Many bars and some restaurants offer tapas, small portions of Spanish and Canarian food, which can either be starters, snacks or combined as a full meal.

---

### Five popular tapas on Lanzarote

*Albóndigas* (meatballs)
*Croquetas* (croquettes), which may be filled with potato or cod
*Gambas* (prawns)
*Pimientos* (peppers), which may be stuffed with a variety of fillings
*Pulpo* (octopus)

---

## Eating out – a practical guide

■ The traditional mealtimes are 1–4pm for lunch and 8–11pm for dinner, though many restaurants are open throughout the day to cater for the varying demands of locals and tourists.

■ If you are happy with the service (see below) leave a tip of between five and ten per cent. In bars leave some small change on the counter.

■ Service is variable. In some local bars in particular, standards of service may appear low (even unacceptably rude) to north Europeans while this is accepted as the norm locally.

■ Booking is rarely necessary except at the smartest or most popular restaurants (noted in the guide under regions). To avoid disappointment it may be worth making a reservation for Saturday dinner or Sunday lunch.

■ It is quite acceptable to order two starters and no main course, or a single starter for two people to share.

■ "Children's menu" generally means fast food or international food. If you want to avoid this, just ask for a smaller portion (*una porción pequeña*) of an adult dish.

■ The café-restaurants in most César Manrique attractions specialise in island dishes, and are usually excellent (there is no restaurant at Cueva de los Verdes, Mirador del Río or the Fundación César Manrique).

■ The only locally owned restaurant chain on the island is Lani's. There are currently 15 branches (nine in Puerto del Carmen, three in the Marina Rubicón at Playa Blanca, two in Puerto Calero and one at Costa Teguise). Most have a stated speciality; for example, Lani's Pizza & Pasta, Lani's Grill, Lani's Tapas, and there is even Lani's Indian Tandoori in Puerto del Carmen. The common theme among all Lani's restaurants is an attractive decor (their trademark is a rustic burned orange and pastel royal blue colour scheme with dark wood), efficient service and a good standard of bistro food at reasonable prices.

**Five vegetarian dishes or tapas**

*Papas arrugadas* with *mojo picón* (► 16)
*Tortilla* (potato omelette)
*Croquetas* (croquettes), which may be filled with potatoes, or
sometimes seafood, so beware
*Pimientos* (peppers), which may be stuffed with a variety of fillings,
so enquire
*Champiñón* (mushrooms), usually stuffed with garlic and fried

## Prices

■ Eating out on Lanzarote is not particularly cheap, as many ingredients
  are shipped or flown into the island.
■ Tapas may seem an inexpensive way of eating, but you may need two
  or three portions to fill up and the price of these can add up to more
  than a conventional meal.
■ Some restaurants offer a fixed price *menú del día*, though this is the
  exception rather than the rule and is more likely to appear at
  lunchtime.
■ By law, service is included in the price, though there may be a
  nominal cover charge for items such as bread and olives or other
  snacks that often appear on the table unrequested.

### A guide to drinking

■ Mineral water is available everywhere. Ask for *agua sin gas* (still) or
  *agua con gas* (sparkling).
■ Coffee is served as *café solo* (a small shot of strong black coffee, like
  an espresso) or *con leche* (with milk). *Café con leche* is usually served
  with steamed milk and is often similar to a cappuccino, though some
  places may simply add warm, or even cold, milk. If you want an
  instant coffee, ask for *un nescafé*. A *baraquillo* is a black coffee with
  a shot of brandy, popular after dinner.
■ Although you will invariably be offered Spanish table wines in most
  restaurants and bars, look out for local wines too (► 19).
■ The local spirit is *ron* (rum), and *ronmiel* (literally honey rum) is a
  popular liqueur.
■ At the end of a meal, many restaurants routinely serve a complimen-
  tary glass of sweet local liqueur.

## Prices

The symbols indicate what you should pay per person for a three-course
meal, excluding drinks and service charge.
€ under €15   €€ €15–25   €€€ €26–30   €€€€ over €30

# Shopping

Despite Spain's membership of the European Union (EU), the Canary
Islands have retained their special status as a free trade zone, with
minimal import duties and a low rate of value added tax (VAT) of 4.5 per
cent. Many everyday and gift items, most notably alcohol, tobacco,
perfume, jewellery and electronic goods, are considerably cheaper here
than in many parts of mainland Europe.

However, because the Canaries are not officially part of the European Union there are strict limits to the amount of goods which can be exported for personal use. The allowances to other European Union countries are one litre of spirits, two litres of wine and either 200 cigarettes or 50 cigars.

## Shopping areas

- The biggest range of shops is to be found in Arrecife and Puerto del Carmen. The capital is the best bet with good-quality Spanish and local brand-name clothes and accessories at prices generally below those of northern Europe.
- Apart from Canarian crafts (►below) and souvenirs, common outlets include surf shops (usually very expensive), perfumers and jewellers and electronics shops selling watches, cameras and high-tech goods all at duty-free prices. The latter are invariably run by Asian traders and prices are almost always negotiable.

## Opening times

- Most shops are open Monday to Saturday from around 9:30/10–1:30 and 4:30/5–8. In the resorts many shops stay open later, until around 10.

## Island wares

- Locally produced goods include basketry, embroidered lace, pottery (often in a heavy naïve style produced without a wheel) and aloe vera products (such as soap, shampoo and skin lotions). Aloe vera is very expensive but also has very good claims to be therapeutic.
- Pieces of pottery and pictures encrusted with island sand and ground volcanic stone are popular. Cheap souvenir shops can rapidly put you off this art form, but when it is well done it can be very effective.
- *Olivina* is a semi-precious lime-green stone formed by volcanic pressure and heat. It is not unique to Lanzarote (in fact larger pieces on sale may well come from Mexico) but it is an island speciality. It is particularly striking when combined with black lava, as is often the case with necklaces.

---

**Island music**

- Despite the numerous music players in its cheap electronics shops, the island has very few CD shops. These are expensive and the latest international tunes take a long time to arrive here.
- If Canarian music gets your toes tapping, look out for *La Gran Antología de la Música Popular Canaria*, a 4-CD set plus book. It's on sale in La Tahona restaurant in Teguise (►69) and at the Tanit Ethnographic Museum shop in San Bartolomé (►86).

---

**Five gifts made in Lanzarote**

- A handmade traditional lady's straw bonnet from Haría market (it will set you back around €40)
- Anything with a César Manrique logo or styling
- A bottle of wine from a local bodega
- A plaque or piece of pottery encrusted with island sand and ground volcanic stone
- Jewellery made from green olivine and/or black lava stone.

- Favourite comestibles include red and green *mojo* sauces, cheese and Canarian wines (usually from Lanzarote). Cuban-style cigars from La Palma are widely available.

## Markets
- The best markets are at Haría on Saturday and Arrecife on Wednesday (both crafts). The island's biggest market is at Teguise on Sunday, which sells just about everything you might want.

# Entertainment

## What's on
- See the local newspaper or pick up a copy of the *Lanzarote Gazette*, which is distributed free in many bars and tourist outlets around the island. They have a very good website, www.gazettelive.com
- *Lancelot* is the island's main foreign-language magazine, on sale in all newsagents and tourist outlets, published monthly in German and quarterly in English, www.lancelot.es
- The tourist office website, www.turismolanzarote.com, has details of local festivals.

## Festivals and folklore
- Fiestas on the island are very colourful and always worth attending (▶ 30). Carnaval (▶ 29) is the biggest festivity, with the most colourful revelries in Puerto del Carmen and Arrecife.
- Folklore shows involve local troupes of singers, musicians and dancers in traditional costume. A characteristic instrument is the *timple*, a ukulele-like 5-string instrument that is unique to the Canaries and is still made by hand in Teguise (▶ 141). Occasionally bouts of *lucha Canaria* (Canarian wrestling) are staged at folklore events.
- Another Canarian folkloric tradition is *juego del palo* (literally, games with sticks), which ranges from using long sturdy poles to vault across gullies and ravines, to sticks as weapons.

## Music
- Don't miss the chance to catch a concert in the Jameos del Agua or the Cueva de los Verdes. As well as occasional concerts this is the second venue for the annual Visual Music Festival of Lanzarote (▶ 60).
- In the capital, occasional concerts take place in the bandstand on the front, the Cultural Centre (opposite) and the Iglesia de San Ginés.

## Bars and clubs
- For visitors, Puerto del Carmen is the nightlife capital of the island, though by the standards of Gran Canaria and Tenerife it is relatively tame. The CC Atlántico on the seafront is the place to go. Costa Teguise is the second liveliest place, with the focus on the Pueblo Marinero and (by coincidence) the CC Atlántico. To see where the locals go for a good time catch the bus to Calle José Antonia, Arrecife, and a taxi back.
- See the "Where to be Entertained" pages, area by area for specific details.

## Sports
- The mild climate and warm seas make Lanzarote a paradise for sports enthusiasts.

## Water sports

- Conditions for windsurfing are among the best you will find anywhere, and world championship events are held annually at Costa Teguise (➤ 74).
- Surfing is also very popular, particularly around Famara (➤ 64, 74).

## Sailing

- The Canary Islands are a halfway point between Europe and the Caribbean, and consequently Lanzarote is a stopover for many international sailors. Puerto Calero is the island's established sailing centre.

## Diving and fishing

- Lanzarote is an excellent dive location. Water temperature ranges from 18°C (64°F) to 25°C (77°F), allowing comfortable diving all year round. The visibility is usually between 30 and 50m (100–165 feet).
- The area around the islands of La Graciosa, Alegranza, Montaña Clara and the smaller islets to the north of Lanzarote makes up the biggest marine reserve in Europe, known as the Reserva Marina del Archipélago Chinijo. The volcanic sea bed is home to diverse flora and fauna including grouper, barracuda, angel shark and moray eel, blue marlin, blue-fin tuna, hammerhead shark, *dorado* (dolphin fish) and local species like *vieja* (parrotfish). In the reefs around the island you can see octopus, anemone, cuttlefish, sea horse and red coral.

## Caves and wrecks

- There are many underwater caves, the most famous of which is the "Cathedral" off Puerto del Carmen, and there are many wrecks for divers to explore. See the excellent report on cave diving on Lanzarote on www.bbc.co.uk/dna/h2g2/A287606
- Bottom fishing is possible all year round for many Canarian species, but the main season for blue marlin and tuna is between April and November (September and October are the best months).
- Many diving and sport-fishing operators work out of the resorts. Puerto Calero is a major centre and the Marina Rubicón at Playa Blanca is up and coming.
- Ask the tourist office for a copy of their *Guia de Actividades Subacuáticas*.

## Other sports

- Keen sportsmen and sportswomen should consider staying at Club La Santa (➤ 26). Club specialities are cycling, aerobics and athletics.
- There is a good golf course at Costa Teguise (➤ 64).
- Several hotels have their own tennis courts.

## Walking

- Lanzarote has no *senderos* (waymarked footpaths). If you're a keen independent walker who can pick up a dusty trail when others are scratching their heads, then go along to the Cultural Department in Arrecife (El Almacén, Calle José Betancourt) where they have a book of walks plus maps for sale.
- The alternative is to join a guided trek. Don't miss a walk in the badlands of Timanfaya National Park (➤ 102–106), Canary Trekking (➤ 9) are highly recommended, and there are walking/trekking specialists in Costa Teguise too.

## Tours and excursions

- These are well marketed all over the island. Ask the tourist office for a copy of *Lanzarote Activa* (an official leisure guide).

# The North

# Getting Your Bearings

The north of the island is home to the island's most spectacular man-made sights, and that man is César Manrique. Devotees can trace much of his life story within the loop that makes up the main roads of the north: his boyhood holidays in Famara; his extraordinary home at Tahiche; his great subterranean garden and belvedere visitor attractions; and even his last resting place in Haría.

The north is not just about one man, though, and there are some stark natural contrasts in a very small area, from the desert-like *jable* around Famara to the lush oasis that is the Haría valley, the stark lichen-covered *malpaís* and the cultivated lava fields around the Monte Corona, and the cactus fields around Guatiza. The north also has the best views on the island, courtesy of its many *miradores* (lookout points).

**The north boasts some of the best views on the island**

There's a contrast in cultures here too, from the Robinson-Crusoe island of La Graciosa to the *centros comerciales* (shopping centres) and "real British pubs" of Costa Teguise. Whatever you do, don't confuse the latter with Teguise, the ancient island capital. Quiet, dignified and lovingly restored, this is possibly the most beautiful small town in the Canaries. If the conquistadors were to come back tomorrow they would still recognise large parts of it.

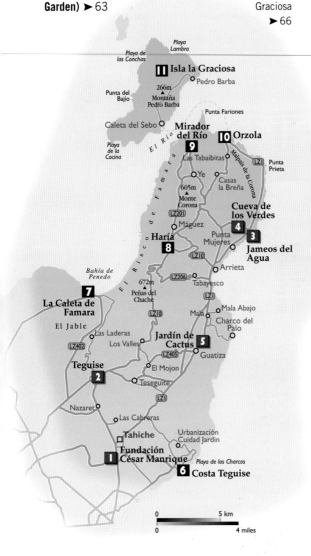

Playa
Lambra

Playa de
las Conchas

**11 Isla la Graciosa**

Pedro Barba

266m
Montáña
Pedro Barba

Punta del
Bajío

Punta Fariones

Caleta del Sebo

**Mirador
del Río**

**9**

**10 Orzola**

Playa
de la
Cocina

El Río

Las Tabaibitas

Malpaís de la Corona

LZ1

Punta
Prieta

Ye

Casas
la Breña

605m
Monte
Corona

**Cueva de
los Verdes**

LZ201

**4**

**3**

Máguez

Punta
Mujeres

**Jameos del
Agua**

**Haría**

**8**

LZ10

Arrieta

El Risco de Famara

Bahía de
Penedo

LZ206

Tabayesco

672m
Peñas del
Chache

LZ1

LZ10

Mala

Mala Abajo

Charco del
Palo

El Jable

Las Laderas

**Jardín de
Cactus**

**5**

LZ402

Los Valles

LZ405

Guatiza

**Teguise**

**2**

El Mojon

Teseguite

LZ1

Nazaret

Las Cabreras

□ Tahiche

Urbanización
Cuidad Jardin

**Fundación
César Manrique**

Playa de los Charcos

**6 Costa Teguise**

0                    5 km
0                    4 miles

# The North in Three Days

## Day One

### Morning

The **1** **Fundación César Manrique** (➤ 54–55) is the perfect introduction to Lanzarote's most influential person. Head north on the LZ10 to **2** **Teguise** (pictured below) and explore its beautiful squares and cobbled alleyways (➤ 56–58). Have lunch here (➤ 68–69).

### Afternoon

Drive up to the Castillo de Santa Bárbara (➤ 57–58) to enjoy great views and to learn about the poignant story of Canarian emigration. Turn off the main road to Teseguite, where you can visit the studios of two of the island's finest artists (➤ 73).

Head north on the LZ1 then turn off to the **5** **Jardín de Cactus** (gateway, pictured opposite, ➤ 63). This is a perfect place for refreshments. If you are too late to eat here (it closes at 5:45pm), the fishing village of Arrieta, 6km (4 miles) further north, has good restaurants (➤ 70).

## Day Two

### Morning

Take the LZ1 and make your first stop the Mirador de los Helechos overlooking "The Valley of 1,000 Palms" (➤ 65). Drive down into **8** **Haría**, browse the shops and have a coffee in its leafy main square (➤ 65). Continue north to the **9** **Mirador del Río** to enjoy the stunning views (➤ 64–65). Return to the main road.

## Afternoon

Head south for 6km (4 miles) and turn off left to the **4 Cueva de los Verdes** (pictured below, ➤ 62) and the **5 Jameos del Agua** (➤ 59–61). It takes an hour to see the Cueva and a little longer for the Jameos but you will be able to get refreshments in a magical setting before you tackle it. If you only have the energy for one, see the Jameos del Agua. Head south on the LZ1. You pass through Arrieta, so if you are still hungry stop off here (➤ 70).

# Day Three

Note: As the weather is unpredictable in the north in the winter, unless you are a keen walker it really is best to visit La Graciosa in the summer.

## Morning

Head straight to **10 Orzola** (➤ 66) to catch the first ferry to **11 Isla la Graciosa** (➤ 66–67) at 10am. Have a quick look around Caleta del Sebo, perhaps an early lunch at El Marinero near the ferry terminal, and either hire bikes or take a taxi to Playa de las Conchas. If you prefer hiking to sunbathing it's quite easy to walk around the whole island, though it is a long way – 19km/12 miles – so allow around six hours.

## Afternoon

Catch the 4pm ferry back and perhaps visit one of the attractions in the north that you may have missed on day one or two. Good meal stops on the return south are Haría (➤ 69) and Teguise (➤ 68–69) on the LZ10 – the long way back – or if you want a fish dinner, choose Orzola (➤ 70) or Arrieta (➤ 70).

# **❶ Fundación César Manrique**

## (Taro de Tahiche/César Manrique House)

In 1966, just after Manrique had returned from America, he was driving past Tahiche when he noticed the top of a fig tree emerging from a huge expanse of petrified lava. He stopped the car, walked over and discovered it had taken root in a *jameo* (▶ 59), or volcanic cave, around 5m (16 feet) in diameter. He noticed there were a further four *jameos* of similar size, and with characteristic resolve determined that this would be the site for his house, to be known as Taro de Tahiche. When he approached the landowner and offered to buy the land he was told it was worthless and he could take as much as he required. This was in fact the perfect challenge and opportunity for Manrique. Here, in the most barren landscape of Lanzarote, he would use its natural features to create a masterpiece, which would show the outside world, and particularly the students who had taunted him at college in Madrid, that the island was much more than just a cinder heap.

The approach is heralded by one of Manrique's most colourful *juegos de vientos* ("wind toys") in the garden.

As you step into the first room of the house and look through the large picture window onto the lunar-like waste ground created by the lava field, you begin to appreciate the extraordinary vision of Manrique. From

**The house and grounds are testament to Manrique's vision and creativity**

his perspective the original landowner's opinion seems to have been fully justified.

The ground floor is a gallery devoted mostly to works by Manrique as well as plans and drawings of his projects. Graphics by other modern masters such as Picasso and Miró are rotated. It is interesting to note the broad range of Manrique's styles, from his early conventional naturalistic works to his later abstract output.

Downstairs is where the real fun is. Curved whitewashed narrow passageways lead from one *jameo* to the next. Furnishings are minimalist, original 1960s chic, and, as at Jameos del Agua (► 59–61), there is a bright blue-and-white painted swimming pool and luxuriant flora.

Manrique lived here until 1988. A victim of his own fame, he moved out to Haría so that he would be less disturbed by casual visitors. Since then, the house has been a visitor attraction administered by the Fundación César Manrique, a body created by Manrique in 1982 in order to promote artistic, environmental and cultural activities.

## No smoking policy

King Hussein of Jordan was an admirer of Manrique, visited Lanzarote regularly, and bought a holiday home here (now the property of the King of Spain). While Manrique was showing him around his house the king took out a cigarette. Although he was indulgent of other people's habits, Manrique never allowed anyone to smoke in his home and, with a smile, asked him to refrain, adding "In this house, I am king!"

Top: The entrance to Taro de Tahiche. Above: César Manrique moved to Lanzarote for the peace and quiet

## TAKING A BREAK

There is a basic refreshment area (smaller than usual at the Manrique attractions). Costa Teguise is 7km (4.5 miles) east, Teguise 6km (4 miles) north, but if you want to stay in the Manrique spirit, head west then north (total 8km/5 miles) to the Monumento al Campesino.

➕ 163 D3 ✉ Taro de Tahiche (just off the roundabout with the giant silver wind mobile) ☎ 928 843 138, www.fcmanrique.org ⏰ Jul–Oct daily 10–7; Nov–Jun Mon–Sat 10–6, Sun 10–3 💰 Expensive

### FUNDACIÓN CÉSAR MANRIQUE: INSIDE INFO

**Don't miss** The much-photographed **giant mural** in the gardens.

# 2 Teguise

The original capital of the island, Teguise is not only the most attractive Spanish colonial town on Lanzarote but the best example of its kind in the archipelago.

Founded in the 15th century, it was the conquistadors' capital and remained so until 1852. The whole town's whitewashed, colonial-style appearance is strictly regulated. Many of its houses have been lovingly restored and are home to top-quality restaurants and shops. Teguise is small, with no modern sprawl attached and very little traffic in its narrow cobblestone streets, so it is an ideal place for strolling (➤ 138–142 for our guided walk).

For six days of the week the town slumbers, then on Sunday thousands of visitors flock here to its tourist market, which takes over the centre. Folklore dancers and musicians perform in the Plaza Miguel beside the handsome Iglesia de Nuestra Señora de Guadalupe.

On the square, guarded by two stone lions, is the Palacio Spínola, built between 1730 and 1780, and now a *casa-museo* (stately home museum) and tourist office complete with chapel, patio and well. A visit will give you a good idea as to how the wealthy citizens of the

On market day La Carpe de Teguise (the big-top circus tent in the square) stages folklore, *lucha Canaria* (Canarian wrestling, ➤ 47), *juego del palo* (➤ 47) plus wine and cheese tasting (€3).

**Teguise is the most attractive Spanish colonial town on Lanzarote**

capital enjoyed life in the 18th century. Also on the square, look inside the rustic stone Caja Canarias bank, which was once the *cilla* or church grain store, built in 1680.

Just off the main square, the adjoining squares of Plaza 18 de Julio and Plaza Clavijo y Fajardo are lined with beautiful historic buildings, now home to shops and restaurants. Just off here is a very picturesque snowy white-topped building with a characteristic outside Canarian balcony. This is the 17th-century Casa Cuartel, formerly an army barracks.

**The church of Nuestra Señora de Guadalupe**

The town has two attractive former convents. The Convento de Santo Domingo has found a new role, housing modern art exhibitions. Between the 16th-century Convento de San Francisco and the Iglesia de Nuestra Señora de Guadalupe, don't miss the Palacio del Marqués, on Calle Marqués de Herrera y Rojas. Built in 1455, it is the oldest building in town and is home to the beautiful Patio del Vino garden bar and café (► 69).

Overlooking the town is the 16th-century Castillo de Santa Bárbara. It sits right on the lip of the Volcán de Guanapay and enjoys 360-degree views. The castle was built as a watchtower but soon became a refuge for the town folk, who fled here to avoid frequent pirate raids. Unfortunately, not everyone could be accommodated here and those left in the town were often

**For richer, for poorer**

Life may have been rosy for the wealthy citizens of Teguise but for the poor folk in the countryside it was anything but, as illustrated by the following quote, which is on display in the museum:
*The days are shrouded by a suffocating blanket of misfortune, which robs us of any hope to carry on.*

The vast majority of emigrants, some 23,000, went to Cuba. Many prospered and received the following accolade from Fidel Castro:
*The Canarian came to work and fight alongside us. He helped forge the country with his proverbial hard work. Our peasants inherited their seriousness, their decency, their sense of honour and also their rebelliousness from the Canarians.*

slaughtered, most savagely in 1586. You can read all about it in the exhibition room at the very top of the castle.

The rest of the castle's dark atmospheric rooms are home to the Museo del Emigrante Canaria (Museum of Canarian Emigration). Quotes and artefacts from ordinary islanders and grainy photographs and documents that go back to the early 19th century make this a fascinating and poignant exhibition.

See how the wealthy lived inside the Palacio Spínola

### TAKING A BREAK

You are spoiled for choice in Teguise (➤ 68–69).

---

🔢 163 D4

**Convento de Santo Domingo**
✉ Calle de Santo Domingo ☎ 928 845 001, www.teguise.com 🕐 Sun–Fri 10–2 💷 Free

**Convento de San Francisco (Sacred Art Museum)**
✉ Plaza de San Francisco www.costateguiseturismo.org
🕐 Sat–Sun 10–3, Mon, Wed–Fri 10–4 💷 Free

**Palacio Spínola**
✉ Plaza de la Constitution ☎ 928 845 181, www.teguise.com 🕐 Sun–Fri 9–4, (Jul, Aug, Sep closed one hour earlier) 💷 Moderate

**Palacio del Marqués** (Patio del Vino, ➤ 69)
✉ Calle Marqués de Iterrera y Rojas ☎ 609 475 043 🕐 Mon–Fri 12–8, Sun 10–3 💷 Free

**Castillo de Santa Bárbara**
✉ 1km (0.6 mile) northeast of Teguise ☎ 928 845 001, www.teguise.com 🕐 Summer daily 10–4, Winter 10–5 💷 Inexpensive

---

## TEGUISE: INSIDE INFO

**Top tip** Come on a Sunday for the **atmosphere** but do visit the shops (they are all open) rather than just patronising the market stalls.

• Regular **buses** run from Costa Teguise (no 11), Puerto del Carmen (no 12), and Playa Blanca (no 13); all departing at 9am and 11am.

• Check out the official Teguise website, **www.teguise.com**, for forthcoming events.

**Don't miss** The **castle** for its intriguing exhibition and wonderful views.

**Ones to miss** The British and German **"home-from-home"** food and drink stalls on market day in the square.

# 3 Jameos del Agua

Regarded by many as César Manrique's most spectacular creation, the Jameos del Agua was also his first tourist centre on the island. Here, two *jameos* ("ha-may-ohs', open-air volcanic caves), and a volcanic tunnel running between them, have been turned into a fantasy grotto. When the Hollywood legend Rita Hayworth visited here in 1966, she declared it "the Eighth Wonder of the World".

You descend stairs into the first *jameo* to find a cool crepuscular café-bar area, luxuriant with tropical plants. Huge lobster pots serve as hanging baskets for giant ferns whose bright green foliage contrasts with the dark volcanic rock. Bird song (natural) and New Age or classical music completes the mood. As your eyes adjust you can see little niches and alcoves that really come into their own in the evenings when this becomes a nightspot (Manrique called it "the most beautiful nightclub in the world").

In the adjoining cave tunnel, there is a perfectly transparent lake. Peer closely and you will see that the still water is populated by hundreds of tiny, almost fluorescent spider-like albino crabs. They once lived deep in the ocean, up to 2,000m (6,500 feet) beneath the waves, but were stranded here long ago and this is the only place in the world where they are now found.

**One of the jameos, complete with "beach" and palm trees**

### What is a *jameo*?

A *jameo* ("ha-may-oh") is a volcanic cave. It is created when the roof of a volcanic tube collapses and lets in the daylight. The raw materials for volcanic tubes are the rivers of lava, which run downhill from an erupting volcano. A tube forms when the outer layer of the lava flow cools and solidifies, but the lava beneath the surface remains hot and continues to flow.

As you emerge up the meandering steps from the dusky tunnel, there is a shock in store. The second *jameo* is a South Seas-style swimming pool, bright blue with a blinding white "beach" (painted stone), picturesque black and grey volcanic rocks and a tall palm tree set at a picture-postcard angle over the pool. Don't bring your swimming costume, as swimming is not permitted (it is said only the King of Spain is allowed to bathe here). At the far end of the pool the final part of the cave system is home to an auditorium seating 600 spectators. It has near-perfect acoustics, is used for folklore shows and concerts and is the setting for the island's annual Visual Music Festival of Lanzarote.

**A cave for concerts (below) and for tiny albino crabs (right)**

Ascend the steps for a great photo opportunity over the pool and you will find a series of rooms housing the Casa de los Volcanes exhibition area and research centre. This is an excellent hands-on introduction to the world of volcanoes and will answer just about any question on vulcanology in Lanzarote, the Canary Islands or indeed worldwide.

### TAKING A BREAK

There are two bars at either end of your visit. The first may be a little too dark for some people. If so, go to the one up the steps above the swimming pool. Both sell snacks, although they are rather expensive.

The restaurant is only open Tue, Fri and Sat evenings and serves top-class island cuisine. Dress code: you must dress smartly (no shorts allowed) in the evenings.

🔲 161 F2 ☎ 928 848 020, www.centrosturisticos.com ⏰ Daily 10–6:30, reopens Tue, Fri, Sat 7pm–2am, Casa de los Volcanes 11–6 💶 Expensive €8, €9

**Restaurant**
☎ 928 848 024 ⏰ Tue, Fri, Sat 8pm–11:30pm 💶 Expensive

## JAMEOS DEL AGUA: INSIDE INFO

**Tip** If you intend visiting the **Cueva de los Verdes** (almost next door, ➤ 62) do that first. It is a very different experience but you may find it an anticlimax if you visit after coming here.
• Keep an eye on **small children** and don't let them run around, as it's easy to stumble in the darkness onto the sharp volcanic rocks.
• Come **late or early** to avoid the tour buses; the last thing you want is a noisy group disturbing the peace!

**In more depth** The **Casa de los Volcanes** is the public face of one of the world's most advanced research and surveillance stations on volcanic activity. The sensitivity of its instruments is mind-boggling; for example its radar satellite pictures can measure a deformation in the Earth (a volcanic precursor) the size of a €1 coin within an 850km (500-mile) radius.

**Don't miss** The opening exhibits of the Casa de los Volcanes; for example, the **"Bubble Tube"** which illustrates perfectly that when the ascending magma reaches a certain level beneath the Earth, the gas within explodes in bubbles erupting through the Earth's crust. There is also some amazing film footage of what happens when the lava reaches the sea.

**One to miss** If you are pushed for time, miss the **upper floor** of the Casa de los Volcanes – by then you may be "volcanoed out" anyway!

# 4 Cueva de los Verdes

You may have visited caves before but probably never one created by molten lava. This is one of the longest lava cave systems in the world.

The Volcán de la Corona (Monte Corona) that created the Jameos del Agua (► 59–61) also created the Cueva de los Verdes (The Green's Cave). It takes its name from a family who once lived here and in the 16th and 17th centuries was regularly used by the islanders as a refuge from pirates and slave traders.

Access to the cave is by a guided tour, taking you on a 2km (1-mile) journey (around 50 mins) through this spectacular labyrinth. It is artfully lit and stairs lead from one gallery to another. The tour ends with a memorable optical illusion.

### TAKING A BREAK

The nearest refreshments are at the Jameos del Agua (around 400m/440 yards away) but you have to pay admission. The nearest recommended alternatives are the fish restaurants at Orzola or Arrieta (► 70).

➕ 161 F3 ☎ 928 848 484, www.centrosturisticos.com ⚫ Daily 10–6 💶 Expensive

## CUEVA DE LOS VERDES: INSIDE INFO

**In more depth** If you want to know how a **lava cave** is formed ► 59–61. This is part of the Atlantida cave system, which stretches for over 7km (4.5 miles) and was formed around 5,000 years ago.

**Top tips** Mind Your Head! You have to **bend low** at several points, and though it may sound obvious some people do emerge from here with nasty bumps.

**Don't miss** The chance to visit a **concert** here. The chamber used for concerts has near perfect acoustics. The world-famous violinist Yehudi Menuhin (1916–99) visited here and gave it his seal of approval. As well as occasional concerts this is a venue for the annual **Visual Music Festival** (► 60).

# 5 Jardín de Cactus (Cactus Garden)

**Putting aside any preconceptions about cacti and even about gardens, this is where nature meets modern art.**

Even the least horticulturally inclined visitor will find this an amazing landscape. Crammed in to the semi-natural

amphitheatre of a former quarry are 10,000 cacti, comprising over 1,100 varieties of all shapes and sizes – spot the fire hydrants, the cauliflower ears, corn cobs, totem poles, giant cucumbers, starfishes and snakes. Dalí-esque fingers of volcanic rock and a windmill complete a surreal scene. It was one of César Manrique's last works and also one of his favourites.

**Prepare to be amazed by the Jardín de Cactus**

### TAKING A BREAK
The café-restaurant here is highly recommended (► 70). Note that your admission ticket entitles you to a free drink here.

🔲 161 E1　☎ 928 529 397, www.centrosturisticos.com　🅒 Daily 10–6 (last admission 5:45pm)　🎫 Moderate (includes a drink)

## JARDÍN DE CACTUS: INSIDE INFO

**Don't miss** Next to the Jardín de Cactus car park an old man with a sign, **Los Cochinillos**, demonstrates just why so many cacti are grown in this part of the island. They attract a parasitic cochineal beetle which when crushed gives a blood-red dye known as carmine (► 23–24). Notwithstanding the fate of the beetles it really looks like human blood on the old man's hands when he crushes them so if you are squeamish be warned.

**Tip** Keep an eye on **small children** and don't let them run around. Stairs are unguarded, surfaces are uneven and the sharp volcanic rocks and cactus spines are both very unforgiving.

**In more depth** If you want to start your own cactus garden, visit the **shop**. They sell cacti (well-packaged) and other good-quality souvenirs and gifts.

# At Your Leisure

## 6 Costa Teguise

This man-made resort, built in 1977, competes with Playa Blanca to be the second biggest on the island after Puerto del Carmen. In the early days César Manrique was a consultant, most notably designing the gardens and pool at the Gran Meliá Salinas hotel (► 71) and the Pueblo Marinero. The latter is a lively square lined with popular restaurants, bars and a bandstand, which is host to live music each night.

Initially it was patronised by the rich and famous, including King Hussein of Jordan and wealthy Spanish residents. Manrique's influence and many of the resort's wealthier clients were lost as subsequent development meant the resort was no longer an exclusive place to stay.

There are three golden beaches, the biggest being Playa de Las Cucharas, which is famous for windsurfing (► 27). Just outside the centre is a waterpark (► 37) and a golf course (► 28).

🔳 163 E3

## 7 La Caleta de Famara

The approach to La Caleta de Famara is called El Morro del Jable (literally, the nose of the sands), a

### Manrique and Famara

César Manrique loved Famara, taking holidays here as a child. One of his unfinished projects was a mirador on top of the cliffs, near the Ermita de las Nieves at Peñas del Chache (► 144, Drive).

barren, windswept plain made up of compacted sand blown across from the Sahara. La Caleta is the little white fishing port, Famara is the beach area just east. To the north the Risco de Famara sea cliffs rise almost sheer to a height of 450m (1,500 feet) and make a magnificent backdrop. In summer its 3km-long (2-mile) golden beach can be a great sight, but in winter the sands turn dull brown and you may not even be able to see the cliffs for mist. Rubbish sometimes washes up here and at any time it is too dangerous to swim. None of which seems to deter the many Norwegian holidaymakers who stay in the Urbanización Famara bungalows behind the beach.

**Haría's pristine white houses and tree-lined streets are some of the most attractive**

Orzola sits at the northern tip of the island

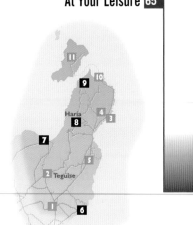

Conditions are excellent for surfing and this is the best beach on the island to learn how to kiteboard (➤ 27–28).

✚ 160 C2

## 8 Haría

This charming, pristine little village of white cubic houses sits in the beautiful "Valley of 1,000 Palms" and frequently invites comparison with a North African oasis. The valley itself, unique in Lanzarote for its plentiful supply of water, is best viewed from one of the *miradores* to the south (➤ 144–146).

The centre of the village is the pretty, pedestrianised avenue-cum-square of Plaza León y Castillo, lined with trees, several restored old houses and the church of Nuestra Señora de la Encarnación. Adjacent is a small Museo de Arte Sacro (Sacred Art Museum).

Haría is a magnet for the art and crafts community and has some good shops. Artisans from all over the island come here on Saturday to participate in Lanzarote's biggest and best craft market (➤ 73). The village was a favourite of César Manrique (➤ 10–12) who lived here from 1988 to 1992. He is buried in a simple grave in the Haría cemetery.

✚ 163 E5

**Museo de Arte Sacro**
✉ Plaza León y Castillo ⏰ Mon–Fri 11–1, 4–6 💷 Inexpensive

## 9 Mirador del Río

Originally the site of a gun battery built in 1898 – during the Spanish-American war – this is probably the most spectacular *mirador* (lookout point) in the whole archipelago. It was carefully designed, by César Manrique (of course!), so that

### Off the beaten track
Just before you get to Orzola you will pass the beautiful white sand beach of Caletón Blanco. A dirt track leads to a small stretch of beach and a lagoon, which is clear, warm and perfect for children.

### Kids' stuff
• Looking at the exotic birds and animals at Guinate Tropical Park (➤ 38)
• Feeding the farmyard animals at Pardelas Parque (➤ 37)
• Splashing about at the Costa Teguise AquaPark (➤ 37)
• Having a go at windsurfing in the sheltered bays for beginners at Costa Teguise
• Swimming in the Caletón Blanco lagoon (➤ see above)

**Relax by the sea in Costa Teguise (top) and Orzola (bottom)**

neither the entrance nor the curvy white stone corridor which takes you into the main room gives you any hint of what is coming next – which is a super-wide angle, almost aerial view, through full-length windows, right across the bright blue straits of El Río to Isla la Graciosa (► below) and the islands beyond. When built in 1973 the Mirador del Río was considered by leading architects to be among the four most prestigious buildings in the world for that year.

You have to go outside to fully appreciate the mirador's jaw-dropping location, set into the side of a cliff face that plummets almost sheer 480m (1,575 feet) to the sea. Down below, the bright pink-, purple- and orange-coloured squares mark the old Salinas del Río saltpans.

 **161 E3** ☎ **928 526 551,** www.centrosturisticos.com 🕐 **Daily 10–5:45** 🖐 **Moderate**

### 🔟 Orzola

Set almost at the northern tip of the island, this little white fishing village, renowned for its restaurants, is the end of the road for most vehicles. However, a dirt track continues north for another 2km (1 mile) to a beautiful golden surfing beach, the Playa de la Cantería. Don't try swimming here, however, as the currents are dangerous.

The La Graciosa ferry runs from Orzola.

✚ **161 E4**

### 🕚 Isla la Graciosa

If you want to get away from it all, this is the place. Around 500 people live on the island and it gets a couple of hundred day-visitors (mainly German) in summer, but with 27sq km (10.5 square miles) to choose from, you can usually find solitude.

The boat docks at the main settlement of Caleta del Sebo, which has a couple of reasonable bar-restaurants and a few basic *pensiones* (bed and breakfasts) if you want to stay overnight. There is a campsite just south of Caleta del Sebo (when

---

**Four troglodyte experiences**
• **Taro de Tahiche:** César Manrique's ingenious home (► 54–55)
• **Jameos del Agua:** the ultimate fantasy grotto (► 59–61)
• **Cueva de los Verdes:** where boiling lava once burrowed its way through the Earth (► 62)
• **LagOmar:** come on a Sunday for cool jazz (► 68)

you arrive, ask at the Oficina Municipal in Caleta del Sebo for permission to camp) and the smaller settlement of Pedro Barba has some upmarket accommodation.

There are several golden beaches around the island, and the gorgeous Playa de las Conchas (6km/4 miles from Caleta del Sebo) is one of the most beautiful in the archipelago; alas, strong currents make it too dangerous to swim from here. To get around the island you can either walk, hire a mountain bike, or take a taxi from Caleta del Sebo, which will bump along the dirt tracks, deposit you at a beach and call back later. There are no hire cars on the island. Conditions on La Graciosa are excellent for scuba diving and fishing.

Island conqueror Jean de Béthencourt (► 13) gave the island its gracious name in thanks for reaching dry land after the long voyage from La Rochelle. He also christened the other islands in the Chinijo Archipelago: Montaña Clara (clear mountain), Alegranza (joy) and the small islet, Roque del Infierno (Hell's Rock). These are all uninhabited and protected as nature reserves.

Getting here: Boats run from Orzola. July–September: departures at 10am, noon, 5pm and 6:30pm (last return 6pm); October–June: departures at 10am, noon and 5pm (last return 4pm). The journey takes 15 minutes.

For more information on the island (in Spanish only) click on www.graciosaonline.com

➕ **161 D4**

**Get away from it all with a trip over to Isla La Graciosa**

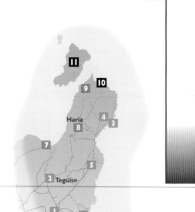

### Hanging out the fish
At Orzola and on La Graciosa you can still see fish pegged on clothes lines, drying in the traditional way.

### LagOmar
This extraordinary bar and restaurant complex, built into the hillside, was designed by César Manrique as a private house and bought by Omar Sharif in the 1970s. It is a favourite haunt of island residents but most visitors never even get to hear of it. If you have already visited Jameos del Agua (► 59–61) you will be familiar with the style.

Legend has it that Omar Sharif lost it in a game of cards. To get there, turn off the main Teguise road at the sign to the Museo and just keep straight ahead, over a roundabout. For a review of the bar and restaurant ► 68. There is also a holiday apartment attached. Click on to www.lag-o-mar.com

# Where to...
# Eat and Drink

## Prices
Expect to pay for a three-course meal for one, excluding drinks and service
€ under €15    €€ €15–25    €€€ €26–30    €€€€ over €30

## NAZARET

### LagOmar €€€

Designed by César Manrique as a private home for Omar Sharif, and recalling the style of Jameos del Agua, LagOmar is built into the face of a cliff, with curving whitewashed corridors linking natural caves and niches. Add plants, unusual artefacts, soft lighting, great tunes and you have a magical bar. Step down from the bar to a landscaped swimming pool and across it to a beautiful modern glass-fronted restaurant serving international cuisine with a French and Italian bias; expect duck magret, salmon en papillotte and desserts. High around the sides of the pool, set into the rock face, are small caves with seats where you can enjoy a romantic drink.

On Sundays they have live jazz. The final bonus is that relatively few island visitors know this place exists. There are two guest cottages available to rent with access to private tennis courts and a swimming pool.

➕ 163 D3 ◻ Cliffs of Nazaret
☎ 928 845 665, www.lag-o-mar.com
🕒 Tue–Sat 12–12, Sun 12–6

bar shares a modern but traditional-style building with two smart shops and an art gallery. It has a courtyard terrace on two levels and plays jazz and chill-out music.

➕ 163 D4 ◻ Calle La Cruz
☎ 928 845 200
🕒 Sun–Fri 11–5

## TEGUISE

### Acatife €€

Acatife (the old name for Teguise) is one of the oldest restaurants on the island. Its pretty, traditionally dark-wood decorated side rooms have pink linen tablecloths and modern art. Among its typical Spanish and Canarian menu, specials include pumpkin soup with a pastry cover, cucumber soup with smoked salmon, sea bream (sama) baked in salt, roast kid and sirloin.

Beware that on Sundays it has something of a split personality, when a couple of its rooms and its main bar area become smoke-filled snack and drinks areas catering for the market crowds.

➕ 163 D4 ◻ Calle San Miguel 4 ☎ 928 845 037 🕒 Tue–Sat 12–4, 7–1am, Sun 9–4

### Bodega Santa Bárbara €–€€

Tucked away behind the church, this pleasant little café-cum-tapas

### La Bodeguita del Medio €–€€

This atmospheric little hole-in-the-wall bar, set in an historic building, is usually spilling out onto the pavement, where its tapas menu is cleverly carved onto wooden tables. It also doubles as a shop selling local delicacies.

➕ 163 D4 ◻ Plaza Clavijo y Fajardo 5
☎ 928 845 680 🕒 Mon–Fri 12–9, Sat–Sun 12–4

### Café Jaleo €–€€

This arty "Culture Café" is set in a charming, traditional, typically Teguisan building with courtyard and serves up tasty tapas, vegetarian specialities and home-made desserts. Every second and fourth Friday, and on occasional Sundays, it hosts live music (jazz, blues, funk...) 🚹 163 D4 ☒ Calle Flores 1 ☎ 928 845 663 ⏲ Sun–Fri 11am–late

### Ikarus €€€

One of the most acclaimed restaurants on the island, this is a place to impress or for special events. The setting is a candlelit 18th-century house gorgeously restored with modern art on the walls. The food is French-international and on the rich side, but rarely fails to please. Start with Ice and Fire (chilled gazpacho and warm avocado), smoked tuna or Guanapay (bacon and chicken liver) salad, then try fillet of lamb with rosemary jus, salmon in saffron sauce, or maybe duck breast in cassis. There is always a good choice of vegetarian dishes too. It's refreshingly unstuffy and the service is very good. 🚹 163 D4 ☒ Plaza del 18 de Julio ☎ 928 845 332 ⏲ Tue–Sat 7pm–late

### Patio del Vino, Palacio del Marqués €€

This exquisite garden courtyard, set in the oldest house in town (▶ 142), is one of the prettiest refreshment spots on the whole island. The German owner is a wine connoisseur and he and his charming staff will encourage you to sample various kinds of fine wine, alongside a selection of top-quality tapas and a number of different island specialities. Alternatively, you can just enjoy a coffee and cake. 🚹 163 D4 ☒ Calle Herrera y Rojas 9 ☎ 928 845 773 ⏲ Mon–Fri 12–8, Sun 9.30–4

### La Tahona €–€€

Locals and tourists rub shoulders in this rustic restaurant-bar almost next to the Convento de Santo Domingo. Go for a good old-fashioned peasant's dish such as pork ribs with corn cobs or Grandmother's beef stew, or typical Canarian favourites such as goat,

*ropa vieja* and *sancocho*. Tapas are also served. 🚹 163 D4 ☒ Calle Santo Domingo 3 ☎ 928 845 892 ⏲ Daily 10–11

## HARÍA

### Casa 'l Cura €€

Satisfying typical Canarian food is served in the small dining rooms which lead off the central bar area of this atmospheric old house. For starters try one of the salads or assorted smoked fish, then try the "pickled" (marinated) pork or fried kid with fried garlic. Sunday specials include chicken soup with noodles and mincemeat, *sancocho*, and fish soup with *gofio*. Finish off with *torrijas con miel* ("bread omelette" with honey). The large dining areas upstairs with picture windows are used by coach parties. 🚹 161 E2 ☒ Calle Nueva (main road to Mirador del Río) ☎ 928 835 556 ⏲ Daily 12–5

### Dos Hermanos €€

Perfectly located in the leafy main square, Dos Hermanos is nearly always busy and is the obvious place to enjoy a leisurely drink while taking in the atmosphere of Haría. If you are tempted to eat here they specialise in fresh fish. 🚹 161 E2 ☒ Plaza León y Castillo ☎ 928 835 409 ⏲ Daily 11–8

### El Cortijo de Haría €€–€€€

This 200-year-old whitewashed farmhouse has been beautifully restored and numerous palms have been planted, which add a sculptural feel. Sit inside the dark traditional cosy rooms or outside on the large sunny terrace under huge shady umbrellas. Suckling pig, roast lamb, rabbit with rosemary and grilled meats are just some of the house specials. 🚹 161 C2 ☒ El Palmeral ☎ 928 835 686; http://restaurante-cortijo.crazy-canary.com (in German only) ⏲ Daily 12–6 (Jul, Aug, Sep 8pm)

## ORZOLA

### Charco Viejo €€

Popular with locals and visitors, this friendly harbourside fish and shellfish restaurant has an open kitchen where you can see the cooks at work. Try the sole, tuna and fish of the day or go for the mixed fish grill.

➕ 161 E4 🗷 Calle La Quemadita 🕾 928 842 591 🕘 Daily 8am–10pm

## ARRIETA

### Casa Miguel €–€€

The bright blue seats of this no-frills, traditional little fish restaurant spill on to the harbour front. Start with the limpets or perhaps fried eel, then try the local fresh fish such as sea bream or *viuda*. There's a choice of meats too, such as goat or rabbit. Ask the waiter about the choice of home-made desserts.

➕ 161 E2 🗷 Calle Garita 🕾 928 848 538 🕘 Tue–Sat 12–7, Sun 12–5

## GUATIZA

### Jardín de Cactus €–€€

If you want a good-quality *al fresco* meal at a very reasonable price with an extraordinary view you won't beat this location (➤ 63). Round wooden tables and director's chairs, set on a raised lava-stone terrace shaded by a large sailcloth awning, provide a very fashionable contemporary feel. Typical Spanish dishes include garlic prawns, marinated pork and *solomillo* (sirloin steak), there are slightly offbeat platters such as Argentine sausage, and excellent value snacks and baguettes. Very good coffee and good service.

Note: You do have to pay the admission price (moderate) to dine here, but it is well worthwhile and the price includes a drink.

➕ 163 C4 🗷 Guatiza 🕾 928 529 397 🕘 Daily 10–4, bar 10–5.45

## COSTA TEGUISE

### El Pescador €€

El Pescador has an unusual interior of elaborately hand-carved wooden panels depicting traditional island scenes, that will either intrigue or disconcert diners. This is one of the best fish and seafood restaurants in Costa Teguise. There is outside seating too, looking onto the lively Plaza Pueblo Marinero. Specialities include zarzuela, paella, cherne in green sauce and king prawns in garlic.

➕ 163 C3 🗷 Plaza Pueblo Marinero 🕾 928 590 874 🕘 Mon–Sat 3–11

### Patio Canario €–€€

Set just off the main part of the Plaza Pueblo Marinero, Patio Canario specialises in tapas and *pinchos* (snacks). Its wooden platters – hams, cheeses, hot kebabs, Iberian meats, Jabugo hams and canapés – are ideal for groups and families. Tapas and *pinchos* start from just €1 so you can afford to try several.

➕ 163 C3 🗷 Plaza Pueblo Marinero 🕾 928 346 234 🕘 Daily 12–12

### La Jordana €€–€€€

Don't be put off by the uninspiring location or bland modern exterior; this stylish restaurant, established more than 20 years ago, is rated among the best in town. It is a favourite of residents and visitors alike and has been frequented by the Spanish royal family and their entourage.

You can either eat in its main dining room, which is rustic and semi-formal, or on its less formal glassed-in terrace. Its long menu is mostly Spanish with some classic international dishes including Burgundy snails and Chicory Roquefort. Specials include fresh local fish, roast meats (including kid and rabbit), salmon Hollandaise and bass supreme.

➕ 163 E3 🗷 CC Lanzarote Bay, Calle Los Geranios 🕾 928 590 328 🕘 Mon–Sat 12–4, 6:30–11:30

# Where to...
## Stay

Prices
Expect to pay per double room, per night
€ under €60    €€ €60–90    €€€ €91–120    €€€€ over €120

## COSTA TEGUISE

### Beatriz Costa and Spa €€€€

You can't miss this huge four-star plus hotel at the far end of the resort. If you like your hotels big and brassy with vast atriums, and if you want the best spa facilities on the island, then this is the place to come. All 349 rooms have either a balcony or terrace with a view of the pool and tropical gardens.

➕ 163 E3 ⊠ Calle Atalaya 3
☎ 928 590 828,
www.beatrizhoteles.com

### Gran Meliá Salinas €€€€

One of the resort's original hotels, Las Salinas was built in the late 1970s and despite recent refurbishment is beginning to look a little dated. This luxury five-star hotel is still one of the best addresses on the island and a member of The Leading Hotels of the World Association. César Manrique designed the murals in the foyer and landscaped the beautiful pool and garden area. All 300-plus rooms look out over the resort's best beach, Playa de Las Cucharas. Facilities include mini

golf, three tennis courts and a Beauty and Wellness Centre.

If you really want to push the boat out, stay in one of the hotel's ten gorgeous romantic garden villas, each with a private swimming pool.

➕ 163 E3 ⊠ Avenida Islas Canarias
16 ☎ 928 590 040, UK 0808 234 1953,
www.solmelia.com

### Mansión Nazaret €€

This charming three-storey aparthotel offers the most characterful accommodation in the resort. The exterior features wrought-iron and dark-wooden typical Canarian balconies. You then enter into a Moderniste (art-nouveau style) hall, and bedrooms and lounges are furnished in rustic late 19th- and early 20th-century style.

There is a lovely swimming pool (heated in winter) bordered by palm trees and plants, and the nearest beach is just 200m (220yards) away.

➕ 163 E3 ⊠ Avda. Islas Canarias 1
☎ 928 590 801, 928 590 416,
www.mansionnazaret.com

### Occidental Grand Teguise Playa €€

Overlooking the small beach of Playa del Jablillo, this popular, recently renovated four-star hotel has 314 rooms, all with terraces, ocean views and most mod cons. It has a lush interior atrium of hanging plants and palms, and the grounds hold two large swimming pools. There is an Italian and a Spanish-Canarian restaurant.

➕ 163 E3 ⊠ Avenida del Jablillo
☎ 928 590 654,
www.occidental-hoteles.com

## LOS VALLES

### Casa El Aljibe €€€

Set in the quiet rural surroundings of Los Valles, this gorgeous rustic holiday accommodation, built into a large high-vaulted subterranean antique water cistern (aljibe), is possibly the nicest conversion on the island. Years of mineral deposits have resulted in beautifully coloured stonework.

The living room (equipped with satellite TV and hi-fi) is in the bottom of the *aljibe*, while the bedroom is on a mezzanine level, set on antique timber rafters. Daylight is funnelled into the interior through high windows. A large, well-appointed kitchen is above ground and looks onto a lovely courtyard and garden shaded by a large fig tree. There is an outdoor jacuzzi and a swimming pool (shared with guests from next door).

⊞ 161 D1 ⊠ Calle San Isidro 72
☎ 928 804 209,
www.lanzaroteisland.com/villas

## HARÍA

### Casa Villa Lola y Juan €€-€€€€

This large farm estate, located in the very centre of the village, nestles among abundant fruit orchards and grapevines and acts as a rural aparthotel offering guests a swimming pool, a solarium with great views of Haría, a tea room and other hotel services.

There are various types of apartment to choose from: two doubles, two suites, one master suite (complete with a hydro-massage bath) and one single-room apartment. All come with a large terrace and are individually decorated with 1930s original and repro furniture. Breakfast is included.

⊞ 161 E2 ⊠ Calle Fajardo 16
☎ 928 835 070,
www.villalolayjuan.com

## YE

### Finca La Corona €€€-€€€€

In the very north of the island under the shadow of the mighty Monte Corona, this is a conversion of an old farming estate into six upmarket holiday homes (five accommodating four people, one accommodating two). It enjoys spectacular views in all directions and is a haven of peace and tranquillity. Each cottage (either one- or two-storey) is a good size, well equipped with spacious marble bathrooms and decorated simply with natural wood. In the lounge is a satellite TV and CD system. Each cottage also has its own terrace-conservatory area. There is a heated swimming pool, a children's pool, barbecue area and mountain bikes to share with other residents.

The surrounding area offers a good supply of local walks including one down to the Playa del Risco, immediately below the Mirador del Río – one of the most attractive and emptiest beaches on the island.

⊞ 161 E3 ⊠ Las Rositas 8
☎ 902 363 318,
www.rural-villas.com

## SÓO

### Casa Blanca €

If you are looking to get away from it all then this pretty guesthouse, located in the hamlet of Sóo on the road to Caleta de Famara, is the perfect place in which to unwind. There are five cosy country-style bedrooms, each sleeping two people. Communal facilities include a swimming pool, tennis court and library and a lounge and kitchen where guests can cook for themselves. Two bathrooms are also shared between guests.

The splendid French hostess and very competent cook, Carole, cooks dinner three nights of the week, and vegetarians are well provided for. Carole is also a qualified guide and takes guests (free of charge) into the Timanfaya National Park. She also has a 12m (39-foot) yacht which guests are welcome to board to discover small bays and look out for dolphins. In addition to all this, she finds time for massage, reflexology, aromatherapy and has a water gym!

⊞ 160 B1 ⊠ Calle de los Parranderos 3 ☎ 928 526 140,
www.lacasablanca.org

# Where to... Shop

## TEGUISE

With its quiet, traffic-free streets and relaxed historic setting, Teguise makes browsing an enjoyable pastime for even the most reluctant shoppers.

Good-quality arts and crafts, jewellery and clothing are the main items. There are few bargains, but many items will be handmade and unique.

**Clothes:** Indigo (opposite the Convento Santo Domingo) has a wide range for women of all ages. La Route des Caravanes (Galería La Villa, Plaza Clavijo y Fajardo 4) sells exotic Moroccan clothing, accessories and household goods.

**Arts and crafts:** On Plaza Maciot de Béthencourt, Tierra, a young co-operative venture, makes some of the best pottery pieces on the island, along with watches and jewellery. Next door, Jerónimo sells funky glass jewellery; Tienda Artesanía Lanzaroteña on the main square has a good range of gifts.

**Antiques:** look in Emporium who have a shop beneath the landmark Casa Cuartel and another, just off the beaten track, in the old cinema on Calle Notas. They specialise in Chinese objects.

Almost next door to the former cinema, Galería Oe makes pieces of sand-and-lava encrusted pottery and large rock-and-sand pictures.

For food and drink try Calzados y Mojos, or Malvasia, on and just off the church square respectively, or the Bodeguita del Medio (▶ 68). Many shops in Teguise close Saturday, but all are open on Sunday.

## HARÍA

In Taller Terrero, on Plaza de la Constitución, you can watch sand-and-volcanic-rock pieces being made. Just along the street is a government-sponsored *artesanía* (handicraft shop). El Palmeral Artesanía is worth a look and La Naturaleza has good clothes and handicrafts.

## COSTA TEGUISE

Shopping here is mostly confined to lacklustre *centros commerciales*. There are branches of Planet and Indigo next to the Pueblo Marinero and a branch of La Tierra inside the square, though it is nowhere near as extensive as the Teguise branch.

## MARKETS

**Costa Teguise** Every Friday night from 6pm till late, there is a craft market in the Pueblo Marinero where you can find a selection of handmade items and novelties.

**Haría** is the venue for the island's largest arts and craft market every Saturday. You can buy basketware, sand-and-volcanic-rock ware, cacti, island wines and foods, lava stone and olivine jewellery. The quality and prices are high.

**Teguise** The Sunday market here is by far the biggest on the island. It attracts bona-fide craftspeople, as well as purveyors of knick-knacks and junk. Goods on sale include leatherwork, clothes, linens, lace, embroidery, ceramics and wooden carvings, in addition to replica football shirts, gaudy beach towels and fake watches.

## Arte Cerámica

It's well worth the short detour to Teseguite (▶ 146) to see the beautiful house and the respective studios of artist Anneliese Guttenberger and potter Stefan Schultz. It's a very friendly place with no sales pressure and even if you don't buy an original there are affordable prints and pieces of pottery. Open Mon–Fri 11–5, tel: 928 845 650, www.aguttenberger.com

# Where to...
# Be Entertained

## NIGHTLIFE

Two of the island's most beautiful and unusual nightspots are in the north the Jameos del Agua (▶ 59–61) and LagOmar (▶ 67), both designed by César Manrique. Dress to impress – no shorts.

The Jameos del Agua and the Cueva de los Verdes also have auditoria where occasional classical concerts and the annual Audio Visual Music Festival are staged. The festival began in 1989, largely as a result of collaboration between island artist Ildefonso Aguilar and British musician Brian Eno.

Costa Teguise nightlife starts in the Pueblo Marinero square, where there is live music and lots of bars. The Avenida Islas Canarias and CC Toca is popular. The Fun Pub Camelot at the CC Punta Jablillo is a decent nightclub.

## WATER SPORTS

The island's best windsurfing conditions are at Costa Teguise, which has been hosting Windsurf World Cup competitions for over a decade.

Two good operators are Windsurf Paradise (tel: 928 346 022, www.windsurflanzarote.com) and Windsurfing Club Nathalie Simon (CNS) (tel: 928 590 731, www.sportaway-lanzarote.com) which also offer surfing, boogie board rental, kayak rental, trekking and mountain biking.

The beach at Famara is the place for surfers and kiteboarders. Famara Surf School caters for beginners and experts. Children can start on boogie boards from the age of nine (tel: 928 528 676, www.famarasurf.com).

Surf San Juan offers surfing for both experts and beginners (Calle Arrufo 5, tel: 928 528 548).

If you want to learn the exciting sport of kitesurfing (▶ 27), contact Costa N-Oeste ("NorOeste") to enrol on their Surf Camp and Kiteboarding Academy (tel: 928 528 597, www.costanoroeste.com).

## DIVING

Diving is very popular at Costa Teguise and dedicated diving schools include: World of Sport & Fun Dive Centre at Calle Marrajo 13 (tel: 928 346 114); Aquatis Diving Center/Diving Lanzarote, on the promenade of Playa de las Cucharas (tel: 928 590 407, www.aquatis-lanzarote.eu); Calipso Diving, Avenida de las Islas Canarias (tel: 928 590 879, www.calipso-diving.com). Native Diving offers diving and surfing, and is based at Hotel Barceló Avenida del Mar (tel: 928 346 096, www.nativediving.com).

Reserva Marina del Archipélago Chinijo (▶ 48), Orzola and La Graciosa are excellent locations for diving and deep-sea fishing. Go with Punta Fariones, based at the Punta Fariones fish restaurant in Orzola (tel: 928 842 558, www.buceolanzarote.com).

## CYCLING

In Costa Teguise, try Tommy's Bike, tel: 928 592 013, www.tommysbike.com. Hot Bike, tel: 928 590 304 or Tracks Mountain Bike Centre, tel: 928 592 028.

The website www.bicyclemania.co.uk is devoted to Lanzarote cycling trails. Canary Trekking (www.canarytrekking.com) organise mountain bike tours of La Graciosa. Bikes may also be hired on the island at Caleta del Sebo.

# The Centre

# Getting Your Bearings

The island capital, Arrecife, and the biggest resort, Puerto del Carmen, dominate the central part of the island. Arrecife, once reviled by tourist guidebooks and locals alike – "crushed by cruel concrete" as César Manrique once put it – is really getting its act together, and a day here, shopping and sightseeing, may well be the most pleasant surprise of your holiday.

Puerto del Carmen wears its heart on its sleeve. Its long sandy beaches and profusion of restaurants, bars, clubs and shops on the promenade, tell you that fun in the sun is what goes down here.

If you want culture, history and sightseeing you have to head out of town to the rural heart of the island. At San Bartolomé and Tiagua, the Museo Etnográfico Tanit and Museo Agrícola El Patio, respectively, tell you all about the old island ways over the last two centuries. A growing number of people are also choosing to make their holiday base here, in the island's stylish *casas rurales* and *hoteles rurales* (country houses and rural hotels).

For a feel of contemporary Lanzarote, hop on the bus to Arrecife, or perhaps take the waterbus to Puerto Calero, where the island's top marina is adding to its attractions and drawing a well-heeled clientele.

**Enjoy shopping in Arrecife (page 75) or lazy beach days in Puerto del Carmen...**

★ **Don't Miss**

**At Your Leisure**

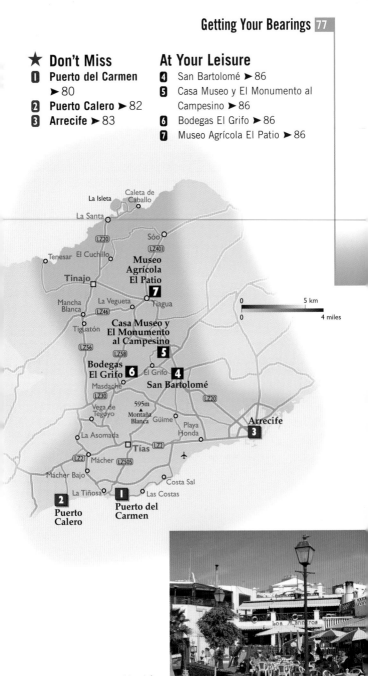

La Isleta
Caleta de Caballo
La Santa

Sóo
(LZ20)
(LZ401)
Tenesar · El Cuchillo
El Cuchillo

**Museo Agrícola El Patio** **7**

**Tinajo**

Mancha Blanca · La Vegueta
(LZ46) · Tiagua

Tiguatón

(LZ56)

**Casa Museo y El Monumento al Campesino** **5**

**Bodegas El Grifo** **6** · El Grifo · **4**
Masdache · **San Bartolomé**
(LZ30)

Vega de Tegoyo · 595m Montaña Blanca · Güime
(LZ20)

La Asomada · Playa Honda
**Tías** (LZ2) · **Arrecife** **3**

(LZ2) · Mácher (LZ505)

Mácher Bajo
Costa Sal

La Tiñosa · **1**
**2** · Las Costas

**Puerto Calero** · **Puerto del Carmen**

0 ———— 5 km
0 ———— 4 miles

...and lunch in harbourside restaurants

# The Centre in Three Days

## Day One

### Morning

Catch the bus to **3 Arrecife**, get off at the Gran Hotel and do the short version of the walk on page 137 which will also allow you to have a good look at the shops before they close at lunchtime. Walk, or take a taxi, to the Castillo de San José (pictured below) where you can browse the modern art collection before enjoying the great sea views over lunch in its acclaimed restaurant.

### Afternoon

Catch the bus back to **1 Puerto del Carmen** (➤ 80–81) and either spend the rest of the afternoon on the beach or get off at the Old Town. Wander down to the port and enjoy a sundowner in one of its many seafront bars or restaurants.

## Day Two

### Morning

Drive to **4 San Bartolomé** and visit the excellent Museo Etnográfico Tanit (➤ 86). Have a quick look at the centre of the town then drive onto the **5 Monumento al Campesino** and have lunch here (➤ 86).

### Afternoon

Continue north to the **7 Museo Agrícola El Patio** at Tiagua (see picture opposite of the windmill, ➤ 86–87). Don't worry if this sounds like a day of museums as the two are quite different and both are very entertaining. Return to the Monumento al Campesino roundabout and head south (right) a short way on the LZ30, which will bring you to the **6 Bodegas El Grifo** (➤ 86).

Sample a couple of the wines (no more if you are the driver), continue southwest on the LZ30 until the turn-off for La Asomada and return to Puerto del Carmen.

# Day Three

(Book a table at the Altamar rooftop restaurant in Arrecife in advance.) Catch the waterbus to **2 Puerto Calero** (➤ 82) and spend a day or half-day excursion on or even underneath the water (➤ 96). If it's a half-day excursion have lunch on the quayside (top) then visit the Whale and Dolphin Museum (➤ 82). Return to Puerto del Carmen and relax on the beach or by the pool.

Catch the bus or taxi into Arrecife. If you have time, have a drink on or just off the promenade then go to the Gran Hotel (➤ 90) and visit the 17th floor to enjoy a meal with a spectacular view of the island by night.

# Puerto del Carmen

The island's biggest and busiest resort, Puerto del Carmen is filled with bars, restaurants and nightspots on its bustling Avenida de las Playas. For a much more charming side, head for the port and the Old Town. The harbour still retains a salty atmosphere with a small picturesque fishing fleet which mixes with the many pleasure craft here, including an express boat service to Fuerteventura (► 40). Next to the harbour a spacious black lava rock square has been landscaped, to include a children's playground and *boules* alleys, and has become a focal point for holidaymakers. On the landward side it is lined with open-fronted bars and restaurants, from which people spill out onto the square on

busy summer nights. The square rises steeply on the far side and a walkway continues around the coast, along the cliff, into the newer part of town. A number of more genteel restaurants sit on this balcony, enjoying the views. Behind the port, a warren of narrow streets ascends swiftly uphill forming the Old Town, served by a handful of local restaurants, bars and shops.

It's a five-minute walk from the port, around the headland, to the landmark Hotel Los Fariones (► 91), which sits in pole position at the start of the Playa Grande beach. The view south, completely unsullied by development, is superb. The view north generally shows a packed beach, lined with blue and orange umbrellas and the backdrop of the Avenida de las Playas, known in tourist parlance as "The Strip". This is the island's biggest concentration of shops, restaurants, bars and

nightclubs, continuing, unabated, cheek by
jowl, for some 3–4km (2–3 miles).

A rocky stretch of around 1km (0.5 miles),
punctuated by two sandy coves, makes the
break between Playa Grande and the town's
second beach, Playa de los Pocillos, which at
1.2km (0.75 miles) long is slightly bigger than
its neighbour. The Strip, which becomes less
concentrated and with less nightlife the
further north you go, finally peters out at the
end of this beach. Beyond, the coast road to
Arrecife is mainly residential, though two
more big hotels sit on the rather empty Playa
Matagorda and brave the noise of
international aircraft to and from
neighbouring Arrecife airport.

## TAKING A BREAK

Puerto del Carmen is chock-a-block with
refreshment options (▶ 88–90).

There are a couple of relaxing little cafés by
the Hotel Los Fariones, or you could pop into
the hotel for a drink in its lovely gardens.

**Playa del Grande** (top) and the old
**port** (left)

✚ 162 B1

# ② Puerto Calero

The island's top marina, Puerto Calero provides berths for over 400 boats, ranging from humble sea cruisers to super-yachts. Most visitors simply use it as a boarding point for a catamaran or submarine trip (➤ 96), but it's a very pleasant excursion in its own right.

A dozen or so restaurants and bars (➤ 89) line the flower-decked quayside and offer a relaxed, elegant waterside setting. Several boats are for charter or offer day trips, including deep-sea fishing and diving (➤ 95–96). The Museum of Canarian Whales and Dolphins opened in 2005 and is dedicated to the 25 types of whales, dolphins and porpoises that swim in these waters. Next door La Galería de Arte showcases the talent of the island's finest artists.

## Getting here
The best way of getting here is to hop aboard the Ana Segundo (Ana II) "express water bus" at the port at Puerto del Carmen. The service departs every hour, costs €7 and takes 15 minutes (tel: 928 514 322). There is also a dedicated Puerto Calero coach excursion which picks up in all resorts three times daily. Tel: 928 513 022 for details.

### TAKING A BREAK
Stop off for refreshment at McSorley's Bar (➤ 89–90), the most popular bar on the seafront.

➕ 162 A1 ☎ For more information on Puerto Calero see www.puertocalero.com

**Museo de Cetáceos de Canarias (Museum of the Canarian Whales and Dolphins)**
☎ 928 849 560, www.museodecetaceos.org ⓞ Daily 10–6, closed first Thu each month 🎫 Expensive

**Galería de Arte**
☎ 928 511 505 ⓞ For exhibitions only Tue–Sat 11–2, 5–9 🎫 Free

The busy marina boasts everything from sea cruisers to super-yachts and catamarans

---

## PUERTO CALERO: INSIDE INFO

**Tips** Forgotten to bring your boat along? Don't worry. Every Friday McSorley's Bar organises a fun regatta and offers enthusiastic sailors on holiday the chance to participate (➤ 95–96).

# ③ Arrecife

Once regarded as little more than a rainy-day shopping option, the capital of the island has smartened itself up immeasurably over recent years and is now a very rewarding excursion whatever the weather. To get the best out of it see our guided walk on pages 134–137.

Arrecife began life around 1403 as the nearest port to the old capital of Teguise (► 56–58). Arrecife means reef and is a natural harbour protected by a barrier of islets and reefs. This, together with its proximity to the rich fishing grounds of North Africa, enabled it to build up the largest fishing fleet in the archipelago. In 1852 it became the capital of Lanzarote. Today it has a population of around 40,000, around 40 per cent of the total island. It has long been the commercial and government centre but made little attempt to attract visitors until a series of major improvements and facelifts began to take place in 1998.

The new centrepiece of the town is its renovated promenade, Avenida La Marina (formerly Avenida General Franco), lined with tropical gardens and a picture-book bandstand (home to the tourist office). Houses spanning several styles and centuries form the backdrop on the town side, while a causeway leads to the town's oldest surviving building, the Castillo de San Gabriel, built in 1590. Formerly

**Castillo de San Gabriel is open for temporary exhibitions**

home to a small archaeological museum, it now stages temporary exhibitions. Almost opposite here, on the seafront, is the Casa de los Arroyos. Built in 1749, it boasts the finest colonial interior in town open to the public, featuring its original courtyard and wooden galleries. It is now home to a permanent exhibition, devoted to the town's famous

physicist Don Blas Cabrera Felipe. The real star, however, is the house itself.

The old-fashioned shops juxtaposed with trendy clothes shops, as well as the mix of architectural styles, make this street ideal for an interesting, leisurely stroll. Or you can simply pull up a chair at one of its pavement cafés, as it's a great place for people-watching too.

Just off here is the picturesque Iglesia de San Ginés, built in 1665. It stands in a very pretty garden square and its beautifully restored interior features late baroque statues of the city's patron saint, San Ginés, and the Virgen del Rosario. Behind here is a large peaceful lagoon, the Charco de San Ginés. This is a lovely spot for a stroll with its old fishermen's houses, boats at anchor and good choice of bars and restaurants.

A little further out, at the end of the port, is the capital's main visitor attraction, the Castillo de San José, built in the

The church of San Ginés (above) has a pretty courtyard and baroque statues. The Castillo de San José (below) is now home to a modern art gallery

late 18th century and restored by César
Manrique to hold the internationally
acclaimed Museo Internacional de Arte
Contemporáneo (MIAC). Works rotate,
but you may spot pieces by Picasso or
Miró and always a Manrique or two. The
contrast between the ancient dark stones
and the vibrant modern artworks is
striking. The castle is also home to one of
the island's finest restaurants (➤ 90).

### TAKING A BREAK

Arrecife is full of good places to eat
and drink. In addition to the places
recommended on page 90, two attractive
café-bars just off Calle de León y Castillo
are the Bar Andalucia 1960, on Calle
Inspector Luis Martin, and La Recova on
Calle Ginés de Castro y Alvarez.

➕ 163 D2

**Museo Internacional de Arte Contemporáneo
(MIAC)**
🏛 Castillo de San José, Avenida de Puerto Naos
☎ 928 812 321, www.centrosturisticos.com
🕐 Daily 11–9 💶 Free

Arrecife has plenty of good places
to eat and drink

# At Your Leisure

## 4 San Bartolomé

This appealing old town is making great efforts to attract visitors by sprucing up its main squares and opening up historic buildings for the first time.

Park anywhere in the centre and have a look at its beautiful main square, a classic Canarian ensemble of parish church, balconied town hall and recently refurbished theatre. Walk through two lower squares and you will come to the Museo Etnográfico Tanit. This is one of Lanzarote's hidden gems, situated in a beautiful 18th-century nobleman's house. Here you can learn almost everything you wish to know about the island's culture, traditions, handicrafts, agriculture and viticulture over the last 200 years. Its many fascinating bygones, ranging from traditional costumes to wine-making equipment, to musical instruments, are beautifully exhibited. The main area is in the house's former wine cellar, but don't miss the chapel or the Princessa Ico room downstairs with its mannequin of a Teguise *diablete* (▶ 29–30).

🔀 162 C3

**Museo Etnográfico Tanit**
✉ Calle Constitución ☎ 928 520 655, www.museotanit.com 🕐 Mon–Sat 10–2 🖐 Moderate €6; children under 12 free

Learn about island traditions at the Museo Etnográfico Tanit

## 5 Casa Museo y El Monumento al Campesino

This bizarre 15m-high (50-foot) Cubist monument marks the very centre of the island and was designed by César Manrique as a tribute to the Lanzarote *campesino* (field worker) for having overcome so much adversity. It is constructed of water tanks from old boats and is said to represent the farmer, his dog and a rat. Beneath it, the much-photographed traditional white buildings are a small part of an old village, restored to house a restaurant (▶ 90). Go through the archway to the right-hand side and you will find a house with an exhibition area and traditional craft shops.

🔀 162 C3 ☎ 928 520 136, www.centrosturisticos.com 🕐 Daily 11–5 🖐 Free

## 6 Bodegas El Grifo

Established in 1775, this charming bodega is the oldest wine cellar in the Canaries, and is still in production today. There is an atmospheric museum located in the original wine cellars with an exhibition of old wine presses, machinery and tools. And, by contrast to most bodegas where you sip a tiny sample of wine while standing up, there is a pleasant rustic bar where you can order wines by the glass or half-glass and sit down in comfort.

🔀 162 B3 ✉ Carretera La Geria-Mozaga (LZ30) ☎ 928 524 951, www.elgrifo.com 🕐 Daily 10:30–6 🖐 Free

## 7 Museo Agrícola El Patio

Established in 1845, Museo Agrícola El Patio is one of the oldest farms on the island still surviving in its original form. Today it is a splendid open-air museum in landscaped gardens.

The farmhouse, now home to part of the Ethnographic Museum, was built in the early 19th century and was inhabited until 1949, when it was the biggest farm on the island, employing 20 workers. There are two windmills here, a beautifully restored picture-postcard *molino* – the conventional freestanding stone variety – and an equally photogenic *molina*, which is a wooden mill housed on top of a building. Between the two windmills a long wooden building houses the rest of the Ethnographic Museum and gives a fascinating insight into rural life during the last two centuries. Don't miss the atmospheric wine museum with its antique bottles and equipment; in the adjacent bodega you can knock back a glass of rough home-made wine and nibble a small tapas (included in the admission price). At its height the farm used 15 camels; now there's just one, a tourist curiosity, corralled with a pair of donkeys.

🔹 162 B4 ✉ Tiagua
☎ 920 529 134,
http://elpatio.turincon.com
🕐 Mon–Fri 10–5:30,
Sat 10–2:30
💶 Moderate €8 (children free)

### Off the beaten track
The Casa del Mayor Guerra just outside San Bartolomé is an imposing nobleman's house built in 1768, formerly home to the military governor. It has been converted to house a museum, a typical Canarian restaurant and artisan's shop.

✉ Located on the outskirts of the village ☎ 928 522 351
🕐 Mon–Sat 10–6 💶 Moderate

### Good places for children
• **Museo Etnográfico Tanit**, San Bartolomé (➤ 86)
• **Whale and Dolphin Museum**, Puerto Calero (➤ 82)
• **Rancho Texas**, just outside Puerto del Carmen (➤ 38)
• **Museo Agrícola El Patio** (➤ below)

Learn about different kinds of windmill at the Museo Agrícola El Patio

# Where to...
# Eat and Drink

## Prices
Expect to pay for a three-course meal for one, excluding drinks and service
€ under €15   €€ €15–25   €€€ €26–30   €€€€ over €30

## PUERTO DEL CARMEN

### Bodega €€–€€€
Bodega has two separate entrances. Pop into its rustic tapas bar for some Iberian pâté with Cumberland sauce, scrambled eggs with king prawns or fried goats' cheese with cranberries, washed down with a glass of the very good house wine. Its main restaurant has a mouth-watering display of steaks, kebabs and other meats. Occasional live music Thursdays.

✚ 162 B1  ⌂ Calle Roque Nublo 3, Old Town  ☎ 928 512 953
⏰ Daily 1pm–midnight

### Bodegón El Sardinero €€–€€€
El Sardinero has two very different restaurants in the port, both of which are recommended for fresh fish. The larger, more formal branch is in the lower square. Its smart dining room is above a very popular bar and has good views onto the port. Specialities include: *xato*, a Catalan salad of cod, anchovies and eggs in *romesco* sauce; carpaccio of tuna; and fish baked in salt.

A few metres uphill, at the start of the row of "balcony" restaurants that look down onto the square, you will find its other branch; small and cosy with red-gingham tablecloths.

✚ 162 B1  ⌂ Calle Tenerife (Upper Restaurant)  ☎ 928 512 128
⌂ Calle Nuestra Señora del Carmen
☎ 928 511 847  928 512 128
⏰ Both daily noon–11

### La Cañada €€€
One of the resort's longest-established and most fêted restaurants, La Cañada has been under the same owner-chef for 20 years.

The setting is formal but rustic and the menu is extensive. House specials include international and local favourites such as brochette of king prawns, sole fillets au gratin on a bed of spinach, fish baked in salt, baked baby lamb, calf filet with pâté and bacon. Lobster thermidor, flambéed steaks, turbot, crayfish and "ox crab" also feature. Finish off with a flambéed dessert.

✚ 162 B1  ⌂ Calle César Manrique
☎ 928 510 415  ⏰ Mon–Sat noon–midnight

### O Botafumeiro €€€
Located at the far end of the Avenida de las Playas, O Botafumeiro is one of the resort's most highly regarded restaurants and specialises in Galician cooking. The shopping-centre setting is not propitious but the dining room is very attractive with tile murals and starched white tablecloths. Start with cream of langoustine soup with armagnac, scallops au gratin or glazed crabs on toast. House specials include Elvers Basque-style, turbot in wine, *cazuela* and lamb. Flambéed dishes are popular. Finish off with Santiago almond cake.

✚ 162 B1  ⌂ CC Costa Luz, Avenida de las Playas (opposite San Antonio Hotel)  ☎ 928 511 503
⏰ Wed–Mon noon–midnight, (kitchen noon–4, 7–midnight).

### Lani's Grill €€
This branch of the popular Lani's chain (➤ 44) is smaller and cosier than its other outlets on The Strip

and has an intimate bodega style of decor, which makes it feel less like an impersonal chain restaurant and more of a friendly neighbourhood establishment. The window display of steaks, kebabs, fish, chicken and burgers is mouth-wateringly tempting and one waft of the grill lures in many a passer-by.

🏠 162 B1 ⊠ Avenida de las Playas/Calle Cenobio
☎ 928 510 020
🕐 Daily 5pm–midnight

## MÁCHER

### La Cabaña €€€€

Darren, the affable owner-chef, hails from Yorkshire, his menu is modern European-Mediterranean and the interior of this charming little restaurant – burned-orange walls with modern artworks – reflects local modern style. Dishes change monthly, but you can expect the likes of roast loin of pork stuffed with fruit and Serrano ham, served with apple mash; poached lobster; or scallops in ginger and onion. Vegetarians can enjoy dishes such as julienne of mixed vegetables in tarragon sauce in puff pastry, or twice-baked Roquefort soufflé with poached pear and walnut salad. Desserts include bread and butter pudding, sticky toffee pudding and lemon tart. There is a maximum of twelve tables, so book early.

🏠 165 E3 ⊠ Carretera Mácher-Yaiza (LZ2) ☎ 646 523 089, 650 685 662 🕐 Mon–Sat 7pm–late

### La Tegala €€€€

This impressive designer restaurant is the brainchild of long-time Lanzarote resident, Antonio Hernandez. His bold, modern, yet still very vernacular building is set high on a hill with fabulous 180-degree views through full-length windows from Arrecife to Fuerteventura. The menu is modern Canarian and Spanish with linen tablecloths, fine china and comfortable leather armchairs. Start with terrine de foie stuffed with Canarian quince jelly and vinaigrette of palm tree honey, feast on grilled Iberian pork with vegetables, sweet potatoes, banana and smoked goat's cheese sauce, and finish with hot soufflé of Valrhona chocolate with cocoa cream and thyme ice cream. For less formal occasions there is an attractive bar where you can choose tapas or light meals, or just have a drink. Whichever, dress to impress!

🏠 165 E3 ⊠ Carretera de Tías a Yaiza, 60 ☎ 928 524 524 🕐 Tue–Sat 2–4:30, 8–11:30, Mon 8–11:30

## PUERTO CALERO

Note: all featured Puerto Calero restaurants are on the quayside

### El Bar del Club (Amura restaurant) €€€€

You can't miss this blinding white building, pointedly set apart from the rest of the quayside restaurants; it resembles a grand mansion from the Deep South of the USA and is the place to come when you really want to push the boat out. The interior is very stylish in a minimal fashion and the menu is nouvelle cuisine with local and Spanish influences. Starters include foie gras, Iberian corn-fed ham, and chilled garlic and almond soup. Mains include parrotfish with limpets and wild mushrooms, crispy suckling pig, wild boar with coconut sauce and creamy black rice. Leave room for the house-special dessert, moist almond sponge cake with thyme ice cream (this needs time to prepare so order it at the start of the meal).

🏠 162 A1 ☎ 928 513 181, www.restauranteamura.com 🕐 Tue–Sun noon–midnight

### McSorley's Bar €

This attractive, nautically themed bar is invariably the busiest place on the front, and attracts a broad range of international customers, from day-trippers just off the Catlanza catamaran to round-the-world yachtsmen. Early Friday evening is the time to be here when the weekly regatta is held (▶ 96) and the bar is bursting at the seams. Good pub grub is served.

🗺 162 A1 ☎ 680 424 665 ⏰ Daily 9am–late

## ARRECIFE

### Castillo de San José €€–€€€

The modern art gallery upstairs (▶ 85) sets the tone for the César Manrique-designed restaurant; a bold statement with stripped wooden floor, black plastic 1960s-style seats (with comfy cushions) and floor-to-ceiling windows giving wonderful sea views. Start with bacon and dates or monkfish and salmon carpaccio, then try *cherne* (stone bass) with king prawns or thyme, or maybe a flambéed steak, and finish with *gofio* ice cream. Cool jazz music complements the sophisticated calm atmosphere.

🗺 163 D2 ☒ Carretera de Puerto Naos ☎ 928 812 321 ⏰ Daily 1–3.45, 7.30–11 (bar open 11am–midnight)

### Emmax €€

Set in a typical single-storey Canarian house, but with a modern, stylish interior, this restaurant-café – opened in 2007 – is already a local favourite. Don't look for paper menus, the choice changes daily and the staff bring freshly chalked blackboards to the table. The cooking is Italian-influenced modern Canarian. Try the black pasta with prawns in an orange sauce if available, sea bass is another good choice (there are always fresh fish options), and the house salad is excellent.

🗺 163 D2 ☒ Avenida Playa Honda 21 ☎ 928 820 917 ⏰ Wed–Mon noon–midnight

### Restaurante (Panorámico) Altamar, Gran Hotel €€€

It's not just the views that you'll enjoy from the 17th floor of this 5-star hotel. Large picture windows and pale wooden floorboards give a real feeling of light and space, and the menu features some of the island's most innovative international-Mediterranean dishes: carpaccio of jumbo prawns with crab butter and calamari noodles; Bilbao-style *dorado*; oxtail in vintage wine with fried beans. It's not cheap, but for a special meal in exceptional surroundings, prices are very reasonable indeed.

🗺 163 D2 ☒ Arrecife Gran Hotel, Parque Islas Canarias ☎ 928 800 000 ⏰ Daily 1–3, 8–11.30

## MOZAGA

### Casa Museo del Campesino Restaurante €€–€€€

Beneath the extraordinary white landmark which marks the centre of the island (▶ 86) is a small rustic-style bodega which serves top-quality Canarian *picoteo* (snacks) such as fried *morcilla dulce* (local black pudding-type sausage) with *mojo verde*, octopus with *mojo picón* and goats' cheese with sweet squares of *gofio* and figs. A large restaurant has been created downstairs, serving a full menu of Canarian specialities.

🗺 162 C3 ☒ San Bartolomé ☎ 928 520 136 ⏰ Daily 1–4

### Caserío de Mozaga €€€

It's well worth the detour to dine in the contemporary country-style whitewashed restaurant in the stables of the old farmhouse. The food is of outstanding quality, combining traditional Canarian and Spanish ingredients and cooking with healthy and modern influences. Start with a salad of langoustines and prawns in papaya and avocado, progress through salt cod in a pepper and garlic sauce, or perhaps a stone-baked entrecote steak, and finish with cinnamon mousse and *biennesabe* sauce. Each plate is a work of art.

🗺 162 C3 ☒ Mozaga ☎ 928 520 060, www.caseriodemozaga.com ⏰ Fri–Sun 1:30–3:30, 7:30–10.30, Mon–Thu 7:30–10:30

# Where to...
## Stay

### Prices
Expect to pay per double room, per night
€ under €60   €€ €60–90   €€€ €91–120   €€€€ over €120

## PUERTO DEL CARMEN

### Hotel Los Fariones €€€
The grand old dame of the resort, the 4-star Los Fariones was built in the 1970s and occupies the best position at the head of Playa Grande. The lounge area and dining room hark back to another era and are comfortable and cosy, in marked contrast with the vogue for echoing spaces found in other resort hotels. The Fariones has its own private secluded sheltered beach, perfect for young children, and the uninterrupted views south, unspoiled by any coastal development, are wonderful. The mature palm-shaded landscaped gardens with swimming pool are beautiful and the food is excellent. The rooms are basic, with no air-conditioning, but they are comfortable. There is a tennis court within the grounds and guests have use of the well-equipped Fariones sports complex across the road which includes a gym, sauna, squash courts, aerobics room, heated swimming pool, five tennis courts and mini-golf. Price includes golf.

🚇 162 B1 🏠 Roque del Este
☎ 928 510 175
www.grupofariones.com

### Los Jameos Playa €€€
Set on the beach at Playa de los Pocillos, this impressive 4-star hotel resembles a very attractive mini-Canarian village with its stone colonial exterior features and wooden balconies, which line the inside of its large central courtyard. This leads onto a large area of mature, palm-shaded gardens where whitewashed buildings are set around lagoon-like swimming pools. Local touches extend to the pretty bedrooms (with air conditioning) and attractive dining rooms. Sporting facilities are very good, with four tennis courts, volleyball, archery, boules, a gym, sauna and beauty centre, mini-golf and courses in diving and tennis. It also has good children's facilities.

🚇 162 B1 🏠 Playa de los Pocillos
☎ 928 511 717,
www.los-jameos-playa.de

### Suite-Hotel Fariones €€€€
Under the same management and next door to the Hotel Los Fariones, these 4-star apartments will suit families who want the location at the head of Playa Grande – though there is no access to the hotel's private beach – and the convenience of self-catering. It is also much cheaper for a family to stay here than in the hotel. There are three pools (one heated in winter), including one for children. Guests can also use the excellent sports facilities opposite the hotel.

A short walk uphill, the Playa Apartamentos Fariones, also under the same management, have fewer facilities on site but are less expensive (€€€). Price includes breakfast.

🚇 162 B1
🏠 Calle Acatife ☎ 928 513 400,
www.grupofariones.com

**Apartamentos Fariones** 🏠 Calle Timanfaya ☎ 928 510 010,
www.grupofariones.com

## PUERTO CALERO

### Costa Calero €€€

If you don't want the bright lights of Puerto del Carmen right outside your window but you do want easy access to its attractions, plus good bars and restaurants within walking distance (Puerto Calero quayside is a three-minute walk away), then this may be just the spot for you.

Opened in 2004, the 4-star Costa Calero is modern, with a large atrium and raw concrete pillars. However, the rooms are smart and comfortable with air conditioning, the food is a reasonable standard, the staff are friendly and the rates here, particularly on promotion, make this one of the best-value hotels on the island. It is consequently very popular, not least with islanders who come here for weekend breaks and to make use of its four pools, sports and leisure facilities (including fitness centre, volleyball, aerobics, table tennis, darts, archery, air rifle shooting and shuffleboard) and its state-of-the-art Thalassotherapy and Wellness Centre.

✚ 162 A1  ⌑ Puerto Calero
☎ 928 849 595, www.iberostar.com

## ARRECIFE

### Gran Hotel €€€

The only high-rise building on the island, the luxurious 5-star Gran Hotel has a very chequered history (▶85). It has now been transformed from the villain of the piece to being a bold and thrusting symbol of the city's current ambition to attract new visitors and business. Rooms and public areas are cutting-edge modern and the main attractions are the state-of-the-art spa and the stunning views from the 17th-floor Altamar restaurant (▶90).

It's also worth noting that while few tourists use this hotel at present there is a good beach right outside which has just been re-landscaped.

✚ 169 A1  ⌑ Parque Islas Canarias
☎ 928 800 000,
www.arrecifehoteles.com

### La Quinta Boutique Hotel €€€

This 5-star villa is in one of the city's most prestigious suburbs, just over 1km (0.6 mile) south of the Gran Hotel. It is not right on the coast but has views of El Cable beach. Decor is very elegant, blending contemporary and classic styles, with antiques in public areas and bedrooms. The dining room and bar lounge are particularly pleasant and you can expect a high standard of cooking. Service is very personal; if you wish, they will even unpack and pack your suitcases! There is a swimming pool in black-lava landscaped gardens and a children's pool too, though this is the sort of place where little ones are best seen and not heard.

✚ 163 D2  ⌑ Calle Hermanos Díaz Rijo, Urbanización La Bufona
☎ 928 810 605

## LA ASOMADA

### Casa Gaida €€€

Although Casa Gaida is situated well inland it enjoys panoramic views of the southern coast overlooking Arrecife, Puerto del Carmen and Puerto Calero, with Fuerteventura in the distance. The house sits within a 14ha (34-acre) estate and is some 200 hundred years old, featuring beautiful traditional interiors of wood and lava stone. It has a fully fitted kitchen and luxurious lounge and dining room with sweeping views. The swimming pool is solar heated and completely private.

✚ 162 A2  ⌑ Camino La Caldereta 52  ☎ 928 832 531, 696 982 882,
www.casagaida.com

### Caserío de Mozaga €€€

Caserío de Mozaga was built at the end of the 18th century. It has been lovingly restored and is now a pristine small hotel beautifully decorated in a simple style with traditional furniture. There are eight double rooms, two of them with a private lounge; all are en suite, offer internet connection, mini bar, satellite TV and hairdryer.

The restaurant is particularly attractive and serves top-quality and appetising Spanish cuisine. Breakfast is included.

**🚹 162 C3 🖂 Mozaga 8
☎ 928 520 060**

## Finca de la Florida €

A cross between a *casa rural* (country house) and a small mainstream hotel, the Finca de la Florida lacks some of the old-fashioned charm of a traditional *casa rural* but it does have many more facilities and is suited to families for whom a beach on the doorstep is not a priority.

There are 15 double rooms (plus one suite) with mini bar, air-conditioning and hairdryer. Facilities include a swimming pool, a tennis court, mountain bikes, gym and sauna, mini-golf, table tennis and a children's playground. Weekly treks are also organised (subject to numbers).

The restaurant (open to the public) is well regarded for its typical Canarian and international cuisine, and enjoys views across the vineyards. After dinner there is a comfy lounge with an open fire where you can have a drink and relax to the sound of classical music.

**🚹 162 C3 🖂 El Islote, 90 San Bartolomé ☎ 928 521 124, 928 521 136.
www.hotelfincadeflorida.com**

## Hesperia Lanzarote €€€€

Opened May 2003, the 5-star Hesperia Lanzarote is a real haven of luxury and in time should become one of Lanzarote's most sought-after hotels. Located on the seafront very close to the marina, its main strengths are its spa and wellness centre and its gourmet restaurant, La Caleta (it also offers two other restaurants). The location, at the far end of Puerto Calero, is away from it all, and if you want to be pampered in peace this is as good a place as any on the island. There are three pools, a fitness room, tennis and squash courts and a putting green.

**🚹 162 C3 🖂 Urbanización Cortijo Viejo ☎ 828 080 800.
www.hesperia-lanzarote.com**

## Tomaren Centre of Holistic Holidays €–€€

Set on a delightful 11ha (27-acre) estate, Tomaren is divided into five houses, one of which is dormitory style (ideal for large families or small groups) and two two-person studios. All accommodation has been restored and refurbished in a rustic, traditional style with natural terracotta floors, ceilings with old beams and volcanic stone walls. Some have good kitchen facilities, but the owners also cook organic meals served in the old bodega cellar.

There is a very impressive large yoga hall, but you will find that all the spaces in this centre have been created with meditation and relaxation in mind. The grounds contain numerous endemic and tropical plants and flowers, organic vegetable gardens, fruit trees, a herb garden, spacious grassy gardens, even two statues of Buddha! Two natural volcanic depressions have been used to create a jacuzzi and an unusual swimming pool.

There is an Inipi (American Indian Sweat Lodge), a steam room and massage and treatment rooms where the owners offer a whole range of natural therapies. Every Wednesday there is traditional Hindu dance, and the owners also organise trekking, surfing and horse riding.

**🚹 162 C3 🖂 Calle Tomaren 33
☎ 676 453 008, 928 520 818,
☎ www.tomaren.com**

# Where to... Shop

## PUERTO DEL CARMEN

The Biosfera Plaza, a short walk uphill from the port or the Hotel Los Fariones, is the best shopping centre in Puerto del Carmen. This attractive, modern mall includes Spanish and international mainstream fashion shops such as Zara, Pull & Bear, Timberland and Footlocker. There is an Artesanía Canaria stall selling handmade goods from Lanzarote, Arteberita with unusual island-inspired artworks, and Natura, which offers items from around the globe. If you are self-catering, there is a food supermarket here. There are a number of fashionable restaurants and cafés here too. Parking is free. Next to the Plaza, Olala has some unusual gifts and jewellery.

Walk downhill towards the beaches and along the main Avenida de las Playas and you will find many small shops selling cameras, watches and discounted electronic goods. The choice and competition means that prices are as keen here as anywhere on the island, though you will still have to barter to come away with a bargain.

Competition to sell is intensive, so take all after-sales or product performance promises with a large pinch of salt.

On the hill is La Tienda de las Cometas, selling kites of all shapes and sizes. Mystic, beneath La Perla Hotel, sells aloe vera products, Haitian art, stylish silk clothes, ethnic jewellery and accessories.

At the far end of Playa Grande look out for Sazón, selling some lovely jewellery; a branch of Olala, and a César Manrique shop. On the beachfront is a Tienda de Artesanía (government-sponsored handicrafts shop). Go on a little further, to Playa Chica, and you'll find Loco and La Fantasia, both good for jewellery and accessories.

On the road from Puerto del Carmen to Macher, Artisdecor sells attractive contemporary and classic Spanish and island pottery, plates, glassware and general household items.

Puerto Calero features a number of designer clothes shops.

## ARRECIFE

Lanzarote's most comprehensive shopping is here in the capital. The pedestrianised centre includes a wide range of shops that appeal to both islanders and visitors. The main street is Calle León y Castillo and you will find most of the main shops on or just off here (Calle Canalejas has some nice clothes shops). Fashion names you may have heard of include Mango and Planet, but there are plenty of other local stylish clothes and accessories shops that are worth checking out, such as Jack Jones, Vero Moda, Tomás Panasco and La Puerta. Some of them occupy premises that are over a century old, which all adds fun to window shopping. At the far end of León y Castillo, the Atlántico mall includes a Hiper-Dino department store.

Arrecife is at its most attractive on a Wednesday when there is a crafts market on the promenade.

On the main road into Arrecife from Puerto del Carmen is Deiland, the island's biggest mall with around 35 shops, cafés, restaurants, a children's soft play area and a cinema.

## AROUND SAN BARTOLOMÉ

Oenophiles should look in at the shop at Bodegas El Grifo (▶86), which has a good range of wine accessories, as well as a full range of bottles for sale. The Monumento al Campesino (▶86) features a number of artisans' studios, so come here if you are seeking basketware, pottery, embroidery or other island craft souvenirs.

# Where to...
# Be Entertained

## NIGHTLIFE

In Puerto del Carmen nightlife is concentrated on The Strip. It's not very sophisticated but it's usually good-humoured and trouble is rare. The most popular place is the Centro Comercial Atlántico. Here you'll find two of the island's most popular and longest established nightspots, the Waikiki Beach Club and Paradise. Charlie's is good for live music with two bands on every night, and there are a number of gay bars. Other popular nightspots on The Strip are César's and Big Apple. You can dance the night away, as some clubs go on until 6am. There is also the relatively low-key Casino de Lanzarote on The Strip (at No. 12) offering the usual betting games (you must be

over 18 to enter and have proof of identity). It is open nightly until 4am (www.casinodelanzarote.com). If a "Medieval Banquet" with booze-fuelled fun and games is your thing, book yourself in at the none too medieval CC Costa Mar for a "knight to remember", tel: 928 510 769. In a similar vein the Country & Western Night at Rancho Texas (▶ 38) is good for line dancing. The bars at the port are buzzing at night, though there are no clubs here. Good places to catch live music are The Crowded House, Scotch Corner and the Irish Craic 'n' Ceol bar.

Arrecife has some good bars and clubs – try Calle José Antonio Ribera – though these cater only for locals. On Calle José Betancourt, the Cine Buñuel shows art-house

movies, and the adjacent Pablo Ruiz Picasso bar is a buzzing place that occasionally has live music.

## PERFORMING ARTS

The charming little Teatro Municipal in San Bartolomé stages concerts and musicals such as *Jesus Christ Superstar* (in Spanish). In Arrecife occasional concerts are also held in the atmospheric surroundings of the Castillo de San José and the Iglesia de San Ginés (▶ 58).

For details of all the cultural events in the area, visit www.cabildodelanzarote.com (in Spanish only). Alternatively, pick up the Agenda Cultura sheet from the Cultural offices next to the Cine Buñuel or at Calle León y Castillo, 6. You can book tickets here too.

## SPORT

### Water sports

Diving is the main activity on this stretch of the coast, with some

extremely good sites around Puerto del Carmen. Reputable operators include Safari Diving, tel: 928 511 992, www.safaridiving.com; Dive Your Way, tel: 671 619 580, www.diveyourway.de; R C Diving Delfin Club, tel: 928 514 290, www.rcdiving.com. Island Watersports operates from Puerto Calero, tel: 928 511 880, www.divelanzarote.com.

If you don't want to take the full plunge, MA Scuba Diving offers a PADI snorkelling course, as well as full diving tuition, tel: 928 516 915, www.madiving.com.

For parascending and water inflatable rides go to Playa Chica, between the port and the Hotel Fariones. Jet skis can be hired from the port. For both call Paracraft, tel: 619 068 680.

### Deep-sea fishing and sailing

Puerto Calero is the island's top sailing centre, with a mix of locals, whose boats are berthed more or less permanently here, and transatlantic sailors who use Lanzarote as a halfway house between Europe and the Caribbean. Several sailing boats are available for charter or day hire (▶ 82).

Every Friday afternoon McSorley's Bar, on the quayside, organises a fun regatta. It's good to watch but even better if you are able to join in. There are normally around six or seven yachts owned by locals with crews of up to seven members. Each yacht reserves at least one space (free of charge) for enthusiastic sailors on holiday, so if you would like to join up, pop into McSorley's Bar on a Friday afternoon (around 3pm) and ask the bar staff for details. As an extra incentive, the winning crew gets a bottle of champagne! More serious yachtsmen should note that the port also hosts the prestigious annual César Manrique Sailing Trophy each October.

Puerto Calero is also Lanzarote's deep-sea fishing centre, attracting professionals and holidaymakers in search of the Hemingway experience. Tino Garcia is probably the top man in the port with two boats, Mizu I and II (tel: 636 474 000). In 1997 a world-record mako shark (488kg/1,076lb) was caught from Mizu II by an inexperienced British angler.

Another good operator is Tono (tel: 619 229 513, www.tonosportfishing.com), who has been known to land blue marlin in excess of 200kg (440lb). A day's session is relatively inexpensive, with return trip, lunch and drinks costing around €70 per angler, €35 per passenger.

The Puerto Calero Deep-Sea Fishing Trophy is the big event of the calendar and attracts more than 50 boats.

### Sea excursions

There are numerous excursions from Puerto del Carmen and Puerto Calero including trips on two real submarines. Submarine Safaris is the leading operator and dives up to 50m (165 feet) below the waves. A diver attracts shoals of fish with food and there are wrecks to be spotted too (tel: 928 512 898, www.submarinesafaris.com). A free pickup service is provided from most parts of the island.

Glass-bottomed boats include Blue Delfin (tel: 928 51 23 23, www.bluedelfin.com) and the submarine-like Aquascope (tel: 928 514 481).

### Bike hire

Ciclomania in Arrecife are the island experts (they sponsor the Iron Man competition so know a thing or two about endurance). They have a range of bikes for all terrains; Calle Almirante Boado Endeiza 9 (opposite Gran Hotel), tel: 928 817 535, www.ciclomania.es

### Horse riding

There are riding stables just outside Puerto del Carmen: Lanzarote a Caballo, on the main LZ2 to Yaiza, tel: 928 830 038. It caters for experienced riders, beginners and children, and offers beach treks for experienced riders.

### Go karts

There are two circuits: Gran Karting Club, at La Rinconada, 2km (1.2 miles) from the airport just off the LZ2, tel: 619 759 946, www.grankarting.com, and Eurokart San Bartolomé, tel 928 520 022, south of the village below the wind turbines. Both will organise transport from the resorts.

### Other sports

The Centro Deportivo at the Hotel Los Fariones is open to non-guests for a small fee and includes tennis, paddle tennis and squash courts, a fitness and aerobic centre, mini-golf, table tennis and an attractive swimming pool, tel: 928 510 175, www.grupofariones.com

# The South and Timanfaya

# Getting Your Bearings

Although Lanzarote is one complete island of contrasting landscapes and contradictions, nowhere highlights it quite as remarkably as the southern part: from the infernal blasted landscape of Timanfaya's *malpaís* to the orderly houses and gardens of Yaiza; the golden Playas de Papagayo to the cinder vineyards of La Geria; the luxury hotels and urban spread of Playa Blanca to the natural phenomena of El Golfo and Los Hervideros. It's a case of black and white wherever you look.

The Fire Mountains of the Parque Nacional de Timanfaya are the main attraction here. Anyone who has ever imagined what a distant planet might look like, or how the Earth may have appeared at the dawn of time, need wonder no longer. For here it is before your very eyes. All that is missing is dinosaurs and aliens – for that you'll have to watch the films that have been made here. Bordering Timanfaya, a visit to the vineyards of La Geria may sound like an acquired taste. But not only is it the island's most unexpected visual treat, it is a remarkable example of man's ingenuity in the face of utmost adversity.

**The south is a place of real contrasts, from volcanic rock to golden sands**

The saltpans of Janubio are another example of how the islanders have successfully harnessed the elements and in doing so have created a semi-natural work of art. The south can also claim the best beaches on the island. There is nowhere else on Lanzarote that is remotely as beautiful as the Papagayo sands – for that you will have to cross the water to Fuerteventura, and that is recommended too.

Playa de la Madera

Mar de Lava

312m

**Parque Nacional de Timanfaya**

**1**

LZ67

Montañas del Fuego de Timanfaya

Playa del Paso

**El Golfo**

**4**

LZ67

Mar de Lava

Playa de los Clicos

LZ702

LZ704

**Yaiza**

**La Geria 2**

**8**

LZ2

LZ30

Uga

**Los Hervideros 5**

**Salinas de Janubio 6**

La Hoya

Las Casitas

Playa de Janubio

609m
Atalaya de Femés ▲

Las Casitas

Caletón del Rijo

Las Breñas

LZ702

Femés

Valle de Femés

Los Ajaches

Playa Quemada

Punta Gorda

LZ701

**El Rubicón**

Punta Ginés

Costa de Rubicón

LZ2

**Playa Blanca**

**7**

Las Coloradas

Punta Gorda

Montaña Roja

Playa Flamingo

Playa Dorada

Playa del Pozo

**Playas de Papagayo**

Punta Pechiguera

**3**

Punta del Papagayo

0      5 km

0      4 miles

# The South and Timanfaya in Two Days

## Day One

### Morning

Pick a clear sunny day to visit the **❶ Parque Nacional de Timanfaya** (► 102–106) so that you can appreciate all the colours, hues and textures of this amazing landscape. If you want to prepare yourself for the trip, pay a visit to the Centro de Visitantes e Interpretación de Mancha Blanca (► 105). It's only a five-minute drive past the main park entrance and while here you may like to sign up for a guided walk in the park. Alternatively, you can get another park taster at the Camel parade (right, ► 103), just north of Yaiza. Enter the park proper, watch the geothermal gimmickry and take the coach tour. If you're a meat eater and the idea of a volcano-grilled steak appeals, take lunch here. Otherwise make the short journey to Restaurant La Era in **❽ Yaiza** (top right, ► 111).

### Afternoon

Just east of Yaiza, pick up the LZ30, which takes you through the heart of **❷ La Geria** (below, ► 107–108), surely the most unusual wine-growing area on Earth. Stop off at the Bodega La Geria (► 108), have a coffee at Bodega El Chupadero (► 108) and make your final stop Bodegas El Grifo (► 108). By the time you leave here you will be an authority on the wines of Lanzarote!

# Day Two

## Morning

Pack your swimming gear. If you have not already seen La Geria, make your way southwest to Yaiza via the LZ30 and follow the Day 1 afternoon itinerary in reverse.

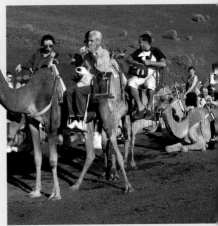

Head from Yaiza to **4 El Golfo** (➤ 110). Visit its amazing emerald lagoon, and if it is lunchtime the village is the perfect place for fish or seafood. If not, wait an hour and you have the whole of **7 Playa Blanca** (➤ 111) from which to choose. Continue along the coast road, pausing to view **5 Los Hervideros** (➤ 110) and **6 Salinas de Janubio** (➤ 110). Continue south to Playa Blanca, make your way to the seafront promenade and continue the salty theme with lunch at the Almacén de la Sal restaurant (➤ 113).

## Afternoon

It's beach time. There's no doubt as to where to go – the **3 Playas de Papagayo** (➤ 109) – the only question is how to get there. The choices are: drive all the way; park near the easternmost hotels then walk; or take the water-taxi from the port (➤ 109). Before you do set off, you may wish to stock up on drinks and snacks. Spend the rest of the afternoon on Lanzarote's best beaches, and return late afternoon to the centre of Playa Blanca where you can shop and enjoy more of its wide range of refreshment options.

# **① Parque Nacional de Timanfaya**

The Timanfaya National Park, or Montañas del Fuego (Fire Mountains), as this area is also called, is one of the most spectacular landscapes on Earth, though Earth will probably be the farthest place from your mind as you gaze upon this scorched and contorted terrain. Its brooding craters and blasted badlands resemble a distant planet. If you only stir once from your beach towel on Lanzarote, make sure it's in this direction.

Start your trip from the Camel Park then enjoy the geothermal demonstrations

## Damage limitation
The reason why the authorities do not allow unsupervised travel within the park is part aesthetic, part environmental, part safety. There is no doubt that the landscape of Timanfaya would certainly lose its otherworldly appeal if there were troops of tourists swarming all over it, but perhaps more importantly it is the fragile landscape that is in danger. Footprints in the volcanic sands here can take years to disappear and there is always the very real possibility of walkers going right through the thin crust of volcanic tunnels that honeycomb the park, causing damage to themselves and the landscape.

The vast majority of visitors approach Timanfaya from the south, and this is the best introduction. The volcanic debris or *malpaís* (literally, badlands) begins just north of Yaiza, and an impish César Manrique-designed devil welcomes you to the outer park area. It is forbidden to leave your vehicle and walk among the *malpaís* (unless supervised by a qualified guide (► below and page 9). Indeed it may look impossible to do so but there are paths – barely discernible to the untrained non-local eye – which are used by locals.

**Most people start from the south side of the park**

There are only two official stopping points in the National Park. The first is at the Echadero de los Camellos ("Camel Park"). This is a chaotic spot, often with dozens of tour buses disgorging passengers into long lines waiting for camels to take them on a short ride up and down the mountain. It's an unusual experience and worthwhile if you haven't ridden a camel before, though this is by no means the most spectacular part of the park. Also here is an information centre and small museum, which includes interesting facts on the traditional use of dromedaries on the island.

Drive a little further on and the entrance to the inner (National) park is on the left. Once past the pay booth, you drive a short way and leave your car next to the Visitor Centre and restaurant. Also designed by Manrique, this belvedere-style building has been likened to the mountaintop eyrie of a James Bond villain, which you will appreciate better as you see it from afar on the coach trip (► 105).

You can walk a little way around the restaurant and take in the views, but you are not allowed to stray far. The area before you, covering just

## Astronauts and cave women
Timanfaya has doubled for the moon and prehistoric Earth. The Apollo mission astronauts were shown pictures of the park to prepare them for their moon landings, and the 1965 Hollywood schlock classic *One Million Years BC* was partly filmed here (► 32).

### Hornitos

This type of curious cowl-like volcanic formation is not uncommon in Lanzarote and is caused when lava is forced up through an opening in the cooled surface of a flow – perhaps by a gas explosion or surface water being boiled – and then accumulates around the opening. Typically, hornitos are steep-sided and form conspicuous domes, pinnacles or stacks. They are fed by lava from the underlying flow instead of from a deeper magma chamber.

It is forbidden to wander unsupervised into the inhospitable *malpaís*

over 50sq km (20 square miles), was mostly created in the first explosive wave of volcanic eruptions that shook the island between 1730 and 1731, though these continued for a total of six years and devastated an area four times this size (► 6–9).

Just in front of the restaurant a park ranger demonstrates that the volcano beneath your feet is still very much alive; a bucket of water is emptied into a tube into the ground and transformed into a scalding geyser; a dry bush is dropped into a fissure and promptly ignites. And in the manner of a schoolboy practical joke, the ranger may scoop up a handful of earth and give it to an unsuspecting person – who quickly releases it with much hand waving! The temperature at ground level is around 100–120°C (212–248°F), at just 13m (43 feet) down temperatures rise to 610°C (1,130°F). The heat is being generated by a live magma chamber some 4–5km (2.5–3 miles) below the surface.

Next to the gift shop coaches depart continuously on the Ruta de los Volcanes (Route of the Volcanoes) tour. This is an unforgettable 35-minute trip taking in the highlights of the central part of the park: a large and photogenic hornito (► box opposite) known as the Widow's Cowl; views inside giant collapsed cones; a stop inside a giant lava canal which has almost become a *jameo* (► 60); the beautiful Valle de la Tranquillidad; and Montaña del Cuervo, the epicentre of the explosions and the most photographed volcano on the island.

**The geothermal demonstrations and the views are awe-inspiring**

A short commentary in different languages accompanies the tour, together with mood music and special sound effects, which are in turn evocative and irritating. The tour ends with the theme tune to *2001: A Space Odyssey*.

## Centro de Visitantes e Interpretación de Mancha Blanca (Visitor Centre)

Around 3km (2 miles) north of the National Park entrance, this visitor centre is designed to answer all your questions about vulcanology on Lanzarote and further afield. It makes a pretty good job of it, with plenty of hands-on stations, but this is better demonstrated at the Casa de los Volcanes at Jameos del Agua (► 59–61).

Watch your food cooking on top of the volcano at El Diablo Restaurant

## TAKING A BREAK

The restaurant enjoys 360-degree views from large glass panels, and the food, which you can see being barbecued on a large grill above the heat of the volcano, is good quality. With so many large parties, however, it's not a relaxing place (tel: 928 840 056 for reservations).

---

✚ 164 C4
**Parque Nacional**
☎ 928 840 057, www.centrosturisticos.com
🕘 Daily 9–5:45, last coach tour 5pm.
Restaurant noon–3:30, café/bar 9–4:45
💷 Expensive €8 (includes coach tours and geothermal demonstrations), children under 12 years free

**Echadero de los Camellos museum-information centre**
🕘 Mon–Fri 9–3 💷 Free; camel rides moderate
**Centro de Visitantes e Interpretación de Mancha Blanca**
☎ 928 840 056 🕘 Daily 9–5
💷 Moderate

## PARQUE NACIONAL DE TIMANFAYA: INSIDE INFO

**Top tips** Make sure you get a **window seat** on the bus. If it looks as if you will be one of the last ones on board, then wait for the next bus and make sure you get in the front of the line for that one.

**In more depth** A **walking tour** into the spectacular central part of the park is led by park rangers and departs (by minibus) from the Mancha Blanca Visitor Centre. It is called the Ruta de Termesana and is very close to where the tour buses go. You must be between 16 and 65 and book in advance; tours run Mon, Wed and Fri, tel: 928 840 839. A **public footpath**, the Ruta del Littoral, follows the coastal path for around 4.5km (3 miles), from just north of El Golfo to the northern tip of the park boundary. You have no choice but to retrace your steps, however, turning it into a 10km/6-mile walk (around five hours). You are allowed to do this walk unaccompanied or you can book a guided tour as above. The tour by Canary Trekking, a company formed by ex-rangers, is longer and quite expensive, but is excellent, tel: 609 537 684, www.canarytrekking.com. See also **Learning more about volcanoes** on page 9.

# 2 La Geria

Bordering the Parque Nacional de Timanfaya, the wine-growing area of La Geria was born out of the volcanic disaster that befell the island in 1730–6. Realising that vines could not only grow but thrive in these conditions – the average yield per vine is around 200kg (440lb) of grapes – the resilient island farmers have not only guaranteed themselves a failsafe crop but have created a unique and visually stunning viticultural landscape (►24–25 and 150).

The black volcanic fields of the valley of La Geria begin at the start of the LZ-30 and straddle the road (to north and south)

as it runs northwest for around 10km (6 miles) or so to Masdache. Along here are several bodegas (wine producers), which are part open to the public and offer

**Bodegas El Grifo Wine Museum (left). Vines grow surprisingly well in the volcanic soil (below)**

### The art of wine engineering

The hypnotic sight of thousands of *zocos* (the horseshoe-shaped vine shelters) flecked with green against a dusky matt black background is for many people the quintessential view of the island landscape. In the 1960s, New York's prestigious Museum of Modern Art featured an exhibit on the area under the title *Engineering without Engineers*.

free samples as an incentive to buy their wine. The best of these are at either end. Near the southeast (Yaiza) end is Bodega La Geria (tel: 928 173 178; pictured below). This atmospheric place is one of the oldest bodegas on the island, established at the end of the 19th century. It is the only bodega to offer guided tours without the need for advance reservation, on Tuesday and Thursday at noon (admission moderate, €5). Still on the main road (LZ-30), at the northwest end of the valley, near Masdache, is Bodegas El Grifo Wine Museum (► below).

The Spanish introduced vines to the Canary Islands, but Lanzarote's characteristic Malvasia grape, which now accounts for 75 per cent of island wines, was brought from Crete in the 18th century. Since then, a unique combination of geology and climate has produced a wine that has won many admirers. Today Lanzarote vineyards are flourishing and produce around two million litres of wine per year. Apart from being carried in visitors' hand luggage, however, this rarely leaves the archipelago.

## TAKING A BREAK

Don't miss Bodega El Chupadero. Unlike the other bodegas mentioned above, it's not a wine producer though it does label and market wine from the locality. Moreover, it is home to a super little restaurant (► 112). The fact that it is "a discovery", albeit only just off the main road, makes it all the more enjoyable.

✚ 162 A2

## LA GERIA: INSIDE INFO

**Top tips** The best place to **buy island wines** is the wine shop at the Monumento al Campesino (► 86). They have a comprehensive range across all major producers and the shopkeeper is very knowledgeable.
• The *malvasia seco* is often rather harsh-tasting, so try a *semi-seco* (medium dry) instead.

**One to miss** Bodega A Suarez if there is a coach party in here.

**In more depth** Pick up the leaflet *Ruta del Vino de Lanzarote* from the tourist office which gives details of where to find the island's other bodegas (Spanish only).
• Visit **Bodegas El Grifo Wine Museum** to see old presses, barrel making and all kinds of antique viniculture artefacts. Daily 10:30–6, tel: 928 524 951, www.elgrifo.com

# 3 Playas de Papagayo

Set right at the southern tip of Lanzarote, the Playas de Papagayo are the best beaches on the island, comprising several coves of gorgeous golden-white sand.

Getting to the beaches by car involves a good 30 minutes of driving (there and back) on bumpy dirt-track roads. To minimise discomfort ignore all signs north of Playa Blanca and instead follow the signs through the resort, along the coast road. The road ends suddenly in a dirt track. Follow this inland and turn right to join the main track into the protected Reserva Natural de los Ajaches, where the beaches are situated. A pay booth is set up here.

A turn-off signposted to Playa Mujeres (and Playa del Pozo) appears 1.3km (0.8 mile) after the pay booth. The first beach you arrive at, Playa Mujeres (2km/1.2 miles after the pay booth), is usually the most crowded. Playa del Pozo and Playas de Papagayo, the prettiest beaches, are reached after another 3.5km (2 miles).

Just past here, around the corner of the promontory, are Caleta del Congrio with its campsite and Puerto Muelas. These are the least attractive but they are relatively secluded and attract nudists.

**Picturesque sands at Playas de Papagayo**

## TAKING A BREAK

There are three cafés, all on the cliffs at Playas de Papagayo. Two of these are very basic. The Oasis de Papagayo with its smart straw umbrellas is very pleasant, but also very expensive.

➕ 164 C1

💷 Admission to Reserva Natural de los Ajaches. Inexpensive

---

## PLAYAS DE PAPAGAYO: INSIDE INFO

**Top tips** To avoid the dirt tracks and the park entrance fee, either get a **"taxi boat"** from the port or park close to the Papagayo Arena Hotel, a five-minute walk from Playa Mujeres. At low tide you can continue walking on the beach all the way to Playas de Papagayo.

# At Your Leisure

## 4 El Golfo

Next to the little white fishing village of El Golfo is one of the island's most curious geological sites and most spectacular beaches. Arriving from the south there are two approaches. The first is signposted Charco de Los Clicos and takes you past a remarkably eroded and striated cliff to a black lava beach and a spectacular rock outcrop. At the back of the beach, half of the El Golfo volcano has fallen away to create an amphitheatre rich in red and orange hues. The star sight is the enclosed lagoon, which has a deep emerald green colour, caused by algae. The best view of the lagoon is actually from above, on the elevated walkway accessed from the village (follow the signpost to El Golfo).

✚ 164 B3

## 5 Los Hervideros

The name translates as the hot springs, and although the water has not been hot here since molten lava

### Off the beaten track

If you are a fan of black beaches try Playa Quemada. The turn-off from the main LZ2 is 3km (2 miles) west after the Puerto Calero turn-off.

*Yaiza is one of Lanzarote's prettiest villages*

tumbled into the sea in 1730–6, the Atlantic certainly boils up, particularly on windy days. Walkways and viewing areas have been cleverly cut into the 15m-high (50-foot) lava cliffs to witness at very close quarters the waves hammering into the shark-tooth caves and whooshing up through blowholes. You may get a little wet but it's all quite safe. One of the island's most popular pictures is taken from here, contrasting the jet-black lava with the bright oranges and purples of the Montaña Bermeja (Purple Mountain) just inland.

✚ 164 B3

## 6 Salinas de Janubio

Saltpans, where seawater is gathered in large chequerboard squares, then left to evaporate, were once common on the island. Today this is the last survivor, and reckoned to be the biggest producer in the archipelago. At its height it employed 200 men; now just 30 work here. The old windmills that you see were once used to pump water into the pans, before being superseded by electric pumps.

There is a restaurant and viewing point from which to contemplate this anachronistic sight. If you manage to see it at dawn or dusk it can be quite magical.

✚ 164 B3

## 7 Playa Blanca

Now one of the island's three biggest resorts, Playa Blanca has grown in leaps and bounds in the last decade, sprawling east and west of the original fishing village which still maintains a likeable low-key atmosphere. The port is home to the main Fuerteventura ferry operators (▶ 40), leisure boats and the vestiges of the town's fishing fleet. From here a very pleasant promenade heads west past the town's seafront bars, restaurants and beach, to the pretty golden crescent of Playa Dorada, dominated by the massive Hotel Princess Yaiza and *centro commercial*.

In the next bay, the Marina Rubicón is the south's answer to Puerto Calero. A newcomer to the marina is Sammer Fine Arts (with galleries in London, Marbella and Madrid). Here, its La Ermita gallery echoes the style of a small island church. It hosts regular exhibitions. Next to the landmark hotel Gran Meliá Volcán Lanzarote (▶ 115), is the Castillo de las Coloradas, a sturdy watchtower built in the 1740s. Beyond large luxury hotels and *urbanizaciónes* have expanded to within touching distance of the protected Papagayo beaches (▶ 109).

➕ 164 B1

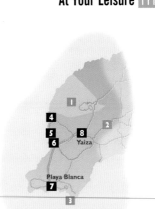

## 8 Yaiza

Often referred to as the prettiest village on the island, Yaiza was

*Playa Blanca has seen rapid growth in the past decade*

settled by wealthy merchants in the 19th century, hence its dazzling white collection of prosperous-looking houses, with best-kept gardens. In the centre is the charming small church of Nuestra Señora de los Remedios, dating from the 18th century. Galerie Yaiza has exhibitions of paintings, ceramics, sculptures and jewellery, most of which are for sale.

Synonymous with the village is the restaurant La Era (▶ 112), one of the most impressively restored 18th-century buildings in the archipelago.

➕ 164 C3

### Good places for children
• The wonderful Papagayo beaches (▶ 109)
• Exploring the nooks and crannies of Los Hervideros, but do keep a close eye on little ones (▶ 110)
• Horse riding at Lanzarote a Caballo (▶ 116)
• Camel riding in Timanfaya (▶ 102–106)

For what's new and happening at the Marina Rubicón, click on www.marinarubicon.com

# Where to...
## Eat and Drink

### Prices

Expect to pay for a three-course meal for one, excluding drinks and service

€ under €15   €€ €15-25   €€€ €26-30   €€€€ over €30

LA GERIA

### Bodega El Chupadero €€

This little gem, deep in the heart of wine country, is only slightly off the beaten track but feels like a real discovery. Given its location, the name is slightly misleading as no wine is made here, though they do bottle and label local vineyards' produce. It's a comfy whitewashed tapas and snacks bar with bright soft cushions, modern art on the walls, friendly staff and delicious food. Try the smoked tuna, the Canarian fresh tomato soup, crêpes with cactus jam or the delicious apple tart. There is a DJ every Friday and occasional live music.

✚ 165 D3 ☒ La Geria ☎ 928 173 115, www.el-chupadero.com
◷ Tue–Sun 11am–late

### YAIZA

### Casona de Yaiza €€€

The cosy rustic restaurant of this boutique hotel (▶ 114) is receiving very good reviews. It is set in the old *lagar* (the room used to house the wine press) with typical whitewashed walls inset with dark lava stones. The menu rotates, offering fine Mediterranean and Canarian cuisine and always a good choice of tapas. Specialities include *arroz negro* (black rice), lobster rice and *fideuada* (noodle seafood paella).

✚ 164 C3 ☒ Calle El Rincón 11
☎ 928 836 262,
www.casonadeyaiza.com
◷ Wed–Mon 1–11

### La Era €€€–€€€€

The most famous place to eat on the island, the multi-award-winning La Era started life in the 17th century as a farmhouse, was beautifully restored by César Manrique in the late 1960s and opened as a restaurant in 1970. It is set in a lovely flower-filled courtyard with a series of rustic cosy dining rooms leading off here. Unfortunately it is not as cheap as it used to be (there is a reasonably priced set menu), but this is still a "must visit" if you want to try the very best in traditional Canarian cooking in a quintessential rustic farmhouse setting. Mainland Spanish specialities are also available. Booking highly recommended.

✚ 164 C3 ☒ Calle El Barranco
☎ 928 830 016, www.la-era.com
◷ Tue–Sun 1–11

### EL GOLFO

### Costa Azul €€

If you want to be on the front row at El Golfo, right next to the crashing waves with the smell of the sea in your nostrils, it has to be Costa Azul. The food, inevitably seafood and fish, is good, but there is no menu and so you are never quite sure how much you are going to pay. The waiters reel off three or four options and you simply choose from that. Locals and expats recommend it and you are unlikely to be ripped off. However, if this doesn't appeal try one of the other restaurants behind Costa Azul; the food is just as good though they don't have the setting.

✚ 164 B3 ☒ Playa del Golfo
☎ 928 173 199 ◷ Thu–Tue 11–10

## PLAYA BLANCA/MARINA RUBICÓN

### El Almacén de la Sal €€€–€€€€

One of the south's most unusual restaurants, the interior of this century-old salt storehouse has been restored with black-painted cast iron, gleaming wood and dark lava stone. A mezzanine floor and a boat "skeleton" slung from the rafters add further interest. The cuisine is a mix of Basque, Galician and Canarian. If you are here for lunch, tables are also laid on the terrace, next to the beach. Live piano music most nights.

➕ 164 B1 ⊠ Avenida Marítima 20
☎ 928 517 885,
www.almacendelasal.com
🕑 Wed–Mon 11–11

### L'Artista €–€€

Set slightly back from the main promenade, this cheerful restaurant is in a lovely old fisherman's house, with a distinctive bright turquoise exterior and attractive colour-washed interior. The menu is typical Italian trattoria fare, home-made pizzas and pastas. Specialities include *carpaccio*, *saltimbocca*, *cartoccio* (fish baked in paper) and *mare e monti* (steak and seafood). On balmy summer nights book a seat on the balcony.

➕ 164 B7 ⊠ Calle La Tegala 18
☎ 928 517 578.
www.pizzerialartista.com
🕑 Mon–Sat 12:30–11:30

### Brisa Marina €€–€€€

One of the best restaurants on the seafront promenade, Brisa Marina occupies a traditional green-and-white nautically themed building with an attractive terrace, beautifully lit by night. It features a long menu of pasta, grilled meats and fish. Specialities include paella, fish in salt and fish soup (24 hours' notice required for the latter).

➕ 164 B1 ⊠ Avenida Marítima
☎ 928 517 206 🕑 Daily 10–9

### Café del Mar €

This is a branch of the near legendary Café del Mar from Ibiza, famous for its chill-out music. Its appearance, however, comes as a surprise – it resembles a 1970s ice-cream parlour, with pastel pink and blue squiggles on a clinical white decor. Once you've got used to this, their squashy white quayside loungers are a good place to hang out while listening to the latest CD music anthology. Breakfasts, snacks and drinks are served.

➕ 164 B1 ⊠ Marina Rubicón,
Playa del Golfo ☎ 928 349 429,
www.cafedelmarmusic.com
🕑 Daily 10am–2am

### Casa Pedro €€

Sailors might rather pull up a seat on the seafront terrace, as the interior of this attractive restaurant is themed on shipwrecks. Start with langoustines in cava or asparagus in Roquefort, then try stone bass in dill sauce, or sole fricassee. For non-fish lovers there is quail, pork loin fillet and double entrecote steak in herb sauce. Finish off with a crêpe suzette or a banana flambé.

➕ 164 B1 ⊠ Avenida Playa Blanca

☎ 928 517 965 🕑 Fri–Wed
noon–midnight

### Casa Roja €€€–€€€€

This sturdy old red-painted house overlooking the waterfront has a restored interior. It describes itself as a "restaurante-pub-snack-cocktail bar" and while you are welcome just for a drink, the food is what Casa Roja is all about. It has attractive wooden terraces upstairs and downstairs.

➕ 164 B1 ⊠ Marina Rubicón
☎ 928 515 886 🕑 Mon–Sat 12–11,
Sun 12–4

### La Giralda €€–€€€

This small elegant informal hacienda-style restaurant on the quayside serves beautifully presented traditional cuisine from Andalucia (and other regions of Spain) in a modern style. Its specialities are its Iberian ham, rice dishes, and grilled and fried fish.

➕ 164 B1 ⊠ Marina Rubicón
☎ 928 519 190,
www.restauranteslagiralda.com/lanza

# Where to... Stay

## Prices
Expect to pay per double room, per night
€ under €60  €€ €60–90  €€€ €91–120  €€€€ over €120

## El Chupadero Bodega apartments €€

Location, location, location are the three magic words here, though it also helps to have the island's nicest wine bar on the premises (▶ 112). Set just off the LZ-30 in the heart of the wine country (▶ 107–108), this former winery has converted part of its building into two holiday homes. One accommodates two people, while the other sleeps up to five. Walls, floors and ceilings are white, and furnishings are a blend of modern and traditional. Both have a kitchen, living room and dining room. The views across La Geria are magnificent, and when the wine bar has closed, the silence is deafening.

🚩 165 D3  ⊠ La Geria  ☎ 928 173 115, www.el-chupadero.com

## Casona de Yaiza €€€–€€€€

The arty boutique-style Casona de Yaiza describes itself as "one of the most beautiful and daring interior decoration projects seen" [on Lanzarote]. Set in an early 19th-century house on the edge of the village with views to Timanfaya, it has eight bedrooms and suites, all individually designed and furnished in rich Italian Renaissance style. Each room or suite is named after a feature of the Fenauso Valley that can be viewed from the hotel. While the decoration in some rooms is quite restrained, others have rather too many cherubs for comfort. All the bathrooms are magnificent and very spacious. The hotel has an excellent restaurant (▶ 112), and downstairs, in a beautifully restored *aljibe* (water cistern), is an art gallery. Outside, guests can relax on the solarium terrace, in the heated swimming pool or in the jacuzzi. Breakfast is included.

🚩 164 C3  ⊠ Calle El Rincón  ☎ 928 836 262, www.casonadeyaiza.com

## Finca de las Salinas €€€

This striking salmon-coloured 18th-century mansion is one of the most prestigious rural hotels on the island. It was the property of a salt merchant and has been refurbished by one of the island's leading architects in a blend of rustic and contemporary styles. Colour-washed walls, often contrasted by bright primary colours, are decorated with modern art and rustic rural objects. The interior is cool and peaceful and palm trees grow up through an opening in the roof. There are 15 bedrooms, all with air conditioning. Guests can enjoy the Finca's wine bar and its Canarian restaurant, and then work off the excess kilos on the tennis court, in the pool or fitness room. There's a jacuzzi, sauna, table tennis and pool table, and the gardens have excellent views of Timanfaya National Park.

🚩 164 C3  ⊠ Calle La Cuesta 17  ☎ 928 830 325, www.fincasalinas.com

## Casa El Morro €€€–€€€€

Built in the 18th century, Casa El Morro is a typical example of the beautiful rural architecture to be found in this wealthy part of the island. It was splendidly restored in 1997, splitting the original estate into five holiday homes, joined by a common patio. There is a lovely swimming pool set among gardens and luxurious terraces with wonderful views over Uga, south towards Femés and towards Timanfaya. The most spacious and attractive of the houses is the two-storey Casa Raquel. It accommodates up to five people and features a private terrace with pergola and a Canarian balcony. The other houses sleep three or four people each. All houses have a living room, kitchen and dining room, satellite TV, radio cassette, coffee machine, toaster and kettle. The decor throughout is rustic, with use of warm teak wood, and the furnishings are cosy and in keeping with the atmosphere.

🚪 165 D3 ✉ Calle El Morro
☎ 928 830 392, 699 417 871,
www.casaelmorro.com

## Finca de Uga €–€€

This charming Casa Rural set on the edge of Timanfaya National Park dates from the beginning of the 20th century. Rooms are in a traditional-minimalist style with "designer" black-lava garden and magical sunset views to the Fire Mountains. Each of its three separate accommodations has its own kitchen and bathroom.

🚪 165 D3 ✉ Calle La Agachadilla 5
☎ 928 836 249, www.fincauga.com

## PLAYA BLANCA

## Casa del Embajador €€€–€€€€

This is a small historic family-run hotel with an entrance right on the promenade. It originally comprised a block of small early 19th-century dwellings, which were bought by an ambassador and converted into a single house. The present owners have made a fine job of restoration and landscaping the grounds in traditional island style. The lounge is very cosy, and the patio where breakfast is served and the outside terrace, with views to Fuerteventura and Isla de Los Lobos, are particularly attractive. There are 12 large twin/ double rooms and one superior suite, each with full sea views, en-suite facilities, satellite TV and mini bar. In the grounds are two tennis courts. Breakfast is included.

🚪 164 B1 ✉ Calle La Tegaia 30
☎ 928 519 191,
www.hotelcasadelembajador.com

## Gran Meliá Volcán Lanzarote €€€€

Set just behind the Marina Rubicon is what appears to be an idyllic little whitewashed village with its own church and volcano. On closer inspection it turns out to be a 5-star-luxe-rated hotel, perhaps the most striking on the island, designed by the well-known architect, A. Piñero. The entrance is through the "church", the "volcano" houses a public area and the hotel's 255 bedrooms are scattered through the Canarian-style "village" bungalow houses. Furnishings and fittings throughout are very tasteful. All rooms enjoy sea views or overlook the main pool area, and have a lounge area. There are four pools in all, plus a well-equipped spa. The hotel sets great store in its gastronomy, with five restaurants including one serving Japanese cuisine. Breakfast is included.

🚪 164 B1 ✉ Urbanización Castillo del Águila ☎ From the UK 0808 234 1953, from Germany 0180 212 1723,
www.solmelia.com

## Timanfaya Palace €€€–€€€€

Set just east of the resort, on the seafront near Playa Flamingo, this large 300-room 4-star hotel is built in an attractive Moorish style with pleasant grounds and an airy interior. It has three swimming pools, a nudist area, an open-air jacuzzi, sauna and gymnasium. Sports facilities include a tennis court, mini-golf, archery, shooting and table tennis. Price includes breakfast.

🚪 164 B1 ✉ Urbanización Montaña Roja ☎ 928 517 676,
www.h10.es

# Where to...
## Shop/
## Be Entertained

## SHOPPING

The main shopping street of Playa Blanca is Calle Limones. For women's clothes try Punta Limones at No 67. Kumal's is a good place for jewellery, handmade porcelain Nao figures and fashion and designer watches.

Chinijos on Calle La Tegala is good for children's clothes. Tienda César Manrique and Mystic, with branches on the promenade and at the Marina Rubicón, are worth a look.

For food, La Era restaurant (▲112) has its own shop and the Ahumaderia de Uga on the main LZ2 sells smoked salmon to the general public, as well as to the island's leading restaurants (closed Monday and Saturday afternoon).

The Marina Rubicón has around 15 outlets, including a handful of designer boutiques with more to follow. Pop into Café del Mar (▲113) to top up your chill-out CD collection.

## NIGHTLIFE

Playa Blanca is a family resort and the nightlife here is pretty low-key. The liveliest place in town is the CC Punta Limones, with Roof Tops being the resort's busiest disco bar. There's live music every night at The Irish Anvil bar at CC Punta Limones, The King's Head, on the waterfront in the town centre, and at

Mollie's Irish Pub at CC Papagayo. For a bit more sophistication head to the Marina Rubicón and hang out at the Café del Mar (▲113).

## SPORT

### Water sports

There are various dive operators. Try the Dive College Lanzarote (tel: 606 853 109, www.scubalanzarote. co.uk), the Diving Center Las Tominas in The Hotel Playa Flamingo (tel: 928 517 300, www.divingtoninas.com), or the Marina Rubicón Diving Center (tel: 928 349 346, www.rubicondiving. com). Also at the marina is Subcat, a hybrid catamaran-submarine which dives up to 25m/80 feet (tel: 928 510 065, www.lanzarote. com/subcat), and Rubisail, a dinghy sailing and windsurfing school (kayaks available for rent from here too, tel: 928 519 012). Various fishing trips run from the port at Playa Blanca. Playa Dorada has water bananas and pedalos.

### Horseriding

Lanzarote a Caballo (tel: 928 830 038, www.alturin.com). 4km (2.5 miles) east of Uga on the main Arrecife road, is a good riding stable that caters for experienced riders and beginners.

## EXCURSIONS

Take to the high seas in style aboard the *Marea Errota*, a reproduction of the classic 19th-century wooden schooner that once plied these waters. The kids can dress up and play pirates, while adults snorkel in the crystal waters off the Papagayo beaches. Tel: 928 517 633, http://personal2.iddeo.es/mareaerrota

Equally eyecatching and much more up-to-date is Segwaytour (Segways are two-wheeled electric scooters) through the Los Ajaches protected park near Playa Blanca; tel: 618 703 463, 625 701 055; www.ajaches.com

# Fuerteventura

# Finding Your Feet

## Getting to Fuerteventura

Regular scheduled boat and express catamaran services run from Playa Blanca and Puerto del Carmen to Corralejo at the northern tip of Fuerteventura.

## Services from Playa Blanca

The huge state-of-the-art *Bocayna Express* catamaran operated by Fred Olsen carries vehicles and foot passengers and takes just 12 minutes to cross the water. The first catamaran to Corralejo leaves at 7:10am Mon–Fri and 8:30am at the weekend. There are departures every 90 minutes to two hours throughout the day. The last boat back from Corralejo is at 7pm. Tel: 902 100 107, www.fredolsen.es. Sample fares: adult foot passenger, return €28; one car plus two adults, return €93.

The *Volcán de Tindaya*, operated by Naviera Armas (➤ 40), also carries vehicles and foot passengers and takes 30 minutes. The first boat to Corralejo leaves at 7am, with regular departures every two hours throughout the day. The last boat back is at 8pm. Tel: 902 456 500, www.navieraarmas.com. Sample fares: adult foot passenger, return €28; one car plus two adults, return €94.

The *Princesa Ico Fuerteventura Express* is a foot passenger-only, glass-bottomed catamaran service from Puerto del Carmen to Corralejo operated by the Princesa Ico company (➤ 40). They offer a free pick-up service from major hotels. It departs at 8:45am daily except Thursday and Sunday and returns 3:15pm. The journey time is 50 minutes and costs €33. Tel: 928 514 322 or 629 731 293, www.princesa-ico.com

## By air

Unless you have a fear of boats or you are perhaps doing business in the two capitals of Arrecife and Puerto del Rosario (close to where the island's respective airports are located), it makes no sense to fly between Lanzarote and Fuerteventura. It takes longer, is more hassle and is much more expensive than going by boat.

### Made in Fuerteventura

- A Fuerte Goat logo T-shirt/bag/other accessory.
- A T-shirt or other item with the island's famous podomorph (stylised footprint) design. These markings are found on the island's sacred mountain, Tindaya.
- Ethnic handmade pottery.
- A *pintadera* – a wooden or pottery stamp block carved with geometric patterns which the ancient Guanches used to tattoo their bodies.

## Organised excursions

In addition to its scheduled ferry services (see opposite), the Princesa Ico company also runs a glass-bottom catamaran, the *Princesa Ico*, on two package excursions from Lanzarote to Fuerteventura. These usually depart from Puerto del Carmen but they may also be put on a service from Playa Blanca.

The Three Island Cruise gives you a couple of hours to visit the shops or market, before re-boarding the boat to visit Isla de Lobos.

The Sand Dunes cruise includes lunch and a bus to the Corralejo dunes. This is of dubious value as you will almost certainly find a better lunch independently and the dunes are only a 10- to 15-minute walk from the centre of town.

For both excursions, Princesa Ico offers a free pick-up service from major hotels. Three Islands departs at 8:45am on Friday, Sand Dunes departs at 8:45am Monday to Wednesday and Saturday. Excursions cost €44 each. Tel: 928 514 322 or 629 731 293, www.princesa-ico.com

*Cesar II* operates an excursion to Corralejo from Playa Blanca.

The major holiday operators also offer Fuerteventura coach tour packages. These have the advantage of a commentary by island guides (make sure they are specialists in Fuerteventura), but the obvious drawbacks of any organised coach tour.

### Playas de Jandía
One of the great features of Fuerteventura is the magnificent long white sandy beaches of Jandía. As these lie approximately 180km (112 miles) south of Corralejo it is not feasible to visit them in a day. Beside which, Corralejo's beautiful beaches are more than adequate.

## When to visit
Corralejo's market days are Monday and Friday. If you want to visit the old island capital of Betancuria, try to avoid Sunday, when most of the attractions are closed.

## Getting about on Fuerteventura
If you intend spending the day in Corralejo then all its attractions are within walking distance. If you need a taxi, they are the same as in Lanzarote, white with a green light on top. If it is illuminated it is for hire. For local journeys fares are metered.

## Exploring the island
If you want to discover more than just Corralejo, you need a car. You can take your own hire car from Lanzarote on the ferry or catamaran from Playa Blanca. If you don't already have a hire car, then you can pick one up at Corralejo from Cabrera Medina, who have an office at the port: tel: 928 517 128, www.cabreramedina.com.

Once out of Corralejo, driving on Fuerteventura is enjoyable, with very little traffic and well-surfaced roads. The only downside is that this encourages fast driving, so be wary of your own speed and that of locals.

Take great care when pulling off the road as the surface is nearly always raised and you can easily damage the underside.

If you do not want to hire a car but still wish to go sightseeing independently then you can catch a taxi from the port. A full-day tour costs around €170 and will get you as far as Betancuria, maybe even La Lajita Oasis Park (▶ 130). Enquire with Corralejo taxis: 928 866 108, or at the Corralejo tourist office (▶ below).

## Tourist information

The information office at Corralejo is at the port. Muelle Chico, Avenida Marítima 2, tel: 928 866 235. Sun–Fri 8–3, Sat 9–12 (closing one hour earlier Jul, Aug, Sep).

For general information on the island see the excellent (unofficial) website, www.fuerteventura.com.

### Isla de Lobos

As long as it is not a windy day, a visit to this beautiful little island is highly recommended. You will find the Lobos ferries just 50m (55 yards) from where the Lanzarote-Fuerteventura boats and catamarans dock. There are only three departures a day, at 9:45, 10:15 and 11:45. It takes 20 minutes to get to Lobos and the fare is inexpensive. The ferry starts coming back at 2:20pm and the last one is around 6pm so you will have time to explore Corralejo's shops, bars and restaurants before getting the Lanzarote ferry.

## Shopping

In general, goods and shops differ little from those on Lanzarote, though there is more choice on Lanzarote. Corralejo is the main tourist shopping town, but there is little here that you won't find in Playa Blanca or Puerto del Carmen. Fuerteventura is famous for windsurfing and surfing and there is an abundance of shops supplying clothes, equipment and accessories.

A general market for visitors tours the island every week and sets out its stalls at the Baku waterfront Monday and Friday (9–1). The goods on sale include leatherwork, clothes, linens, lace, embroidery, ceramics, other handicrafts and the usual cheap knick-knacks (replica football shirts, gaudy beach towels, fake watches, etc). There are some quality items here, though you will have to barter to get a decent price.

## Eating out

There is little variation here from what you will find on Lanzarote. The island speciality is goat, which appears on the menu in just about every conceivable form. All local restaurants feature goats' cheese (*queso de cabra*) among their starters. If it's not served plain with sliced tomatoes, it may be fried in breadcrumbs and served with quince jam (*membrillo*), palm honey (*miel de palma*), or perhaps *mojo verde*. Look out for kid (*cabrito*), which is fried, baked or served in a stew (*compuesta*). Some restaurants only serve goat or kid stew on a Sunday lunchtime.

# Getting Your Bearings

After the tidy lines of Lanzarote, with its beautifully tended designer houses and manicured fields and gardens, the dusty streets and barren landscapes of Fuerteventura come as quite a contrast. Whisper it carefully in Corralejo, but it's rather like setting the clock back, and, once you are out in the countryside, time vanishes altogether.

Corralejo is the island's busiest and most built-up resort, not dissimilar in atmosphere to Playa Blanca and, like Puerto del Carmen, it has a Strip of international bars and shopping centres, albeit a fraction of the size of Puerto's. The town's two big attractions are its magnificent beach, famously backed by a huge expanse of wild dunes, and the Baku waterpark.

If you're more the island explorer type, hire a car and head down to the old capital of Betancuria (➤ 127–128), passing through historic villages en route. After the Fire Mountains of Timanfaya, the volcanic landscapes may be a little tame, but there's no denying that it has a certain grandeur and in places you can drive for miles without seeing another person, let alone a designer restaurant or boutique hotel. Fuerteventura has had no César Manrique-type figurehead to create tourist attractions or pronounce on matters of design, but in best-kept little villages like Villaverde, Betancuria and Pájara you will get a good sense of *majorero* (Fuerteventuran) style.

**A visit to Fuerteventura can be like stepping back in time**

## ★ Don't Miss

1 **Corralejo** ➤ 125
2 **Betancuria** ➤ 127

## At Your Leisure

3 La Oliva ➤ 129
4 Ecomuseo de La Alcogida ➤ 129
5 Antigua ➤ 129
6 La Lajita Oasis Park ➤ 130

Punta Gorda
Punta Blanca
Corralejo 1
FV101
Parque Natural de las Dunas de Corralejo
FV10
El Cotillo
Lajares
309m
FV1
Villaverde
3 La Oliva
399m
Tindaya
FV10
Tetir
FV1
Los Molinos
FV221
Tefía
4 Ecomuseo de La Alcogida
FV3
Llanos de la Concepción
Casillas del Angel
PUERTO DEL ROSARIO
Valle de Santa Inés
La Ampuyenta
FV20
FV2
Triquivijate
Betancuria 2
5 Antigua
Caleta de Fuste
Ajuy
Vega de Río Palmas
FV30
Agua de Bueyes
FV2
Salinas del Carmen
Pájara
Tiscamanita
FV605
Tuineje
FV420
Casas de Pozo Negro
FV2
Tesejerague
FV20
FV512
Las Playitas
La Pared
La Lajita Oasis Park
Giniginámar
Gran Tarajal
Tarajalejo
6
La Lajita
0
10 km
0
8 miles

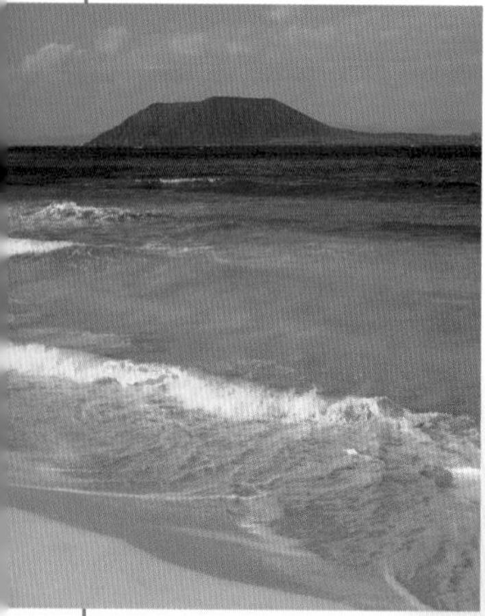

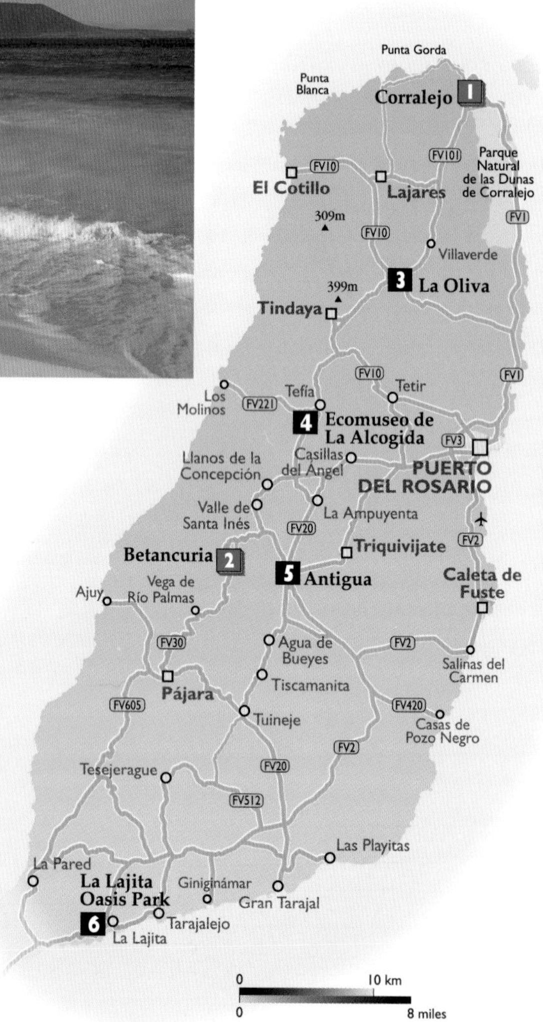

# Fuerteventura in One Day

**Option A: foot passengers only. Market day is Monday and Friday.**

## Morning

Disembark at **1** Corralejo (➤ 125–126), walk straight ahead, and at the end of the port grab a coffee and snack at the café/bakery, La Olá, on the right-hand side. Walk along the pleasant seafront promenade until it ends at the Corralejo Beach hotel. On the other side of this you will find the main shopping street of Avenida Nuestra Señora del Carmen. At the top of here (turn left), the market (➤ 120) is held on Monday and Friday. For lunch visit Ambaradam (➤ 131), at Baku water park.

## Afternoon

Baku (➤ 125), with lots more to offer families besides its watery attraction, could quite easily detain you for the rest of the afternoon. However, it would be a shame not to see the golden sands of Flag Beach and Corralejo's famous dunes. It's a 10- to 15-minute walk along Avenida de Fuerteventura in front of Baku, or you can hail a taxi. Walking is shorter as you can cut the corner. Just follow the seafront and the crowds. This leads back to the seafront promenade and the old town where there is a good choice of restaurants and bars (right) for a quick meal or snack before you catch the boat.

**Option B: Visitors with a car. Avoid Sundays when most of Betancuria's attractions are closed.**

# Morning

Make an early start. From the ❶ port (➤ 126–127) go straight ahead (stop next to La Olá if you want a coffee), fork left into Calle Nuestra Señora del Carmen and continue until you come to a T-junction. Turn left and you are on Corralejo ring road. Follow the signs to La Oliva (18km/11 miles) to pick up the FV101. After 13km (8 miles) you will pass through one of the island's best-kept villages, Villaverde. Go through ❸ **La Oliva** (➤ 129), past Montaña Tindaya (on your right) and after another 10km (6 miles) turn right onto the FV207. After another 7km (4 miles) there is a very good open-air museum, the ❹ **Ecomuseo de La Alcogida** (➤ 129). It serves basic refreshments so you can also use it as a coffee stop. The FV207 ends after another 6km (3.5 miles) at the scenic FV30. Turn right towards ❷ **Betancuria** where you can spend the next two to three hours sightseeing and having lunch (➤ 127–128 and 132).

# Afternoon

Return north on the FV30 for 15km (9 miles) and turn right onto the FV415 to ❺ **Antigua** (above, ➤ 129–130). Turn left in the centre of this pretty village and head north on the FV20 for 1–2km (0.5–1 mile), to see the landmark 200-year-old windmill. With its garden, plaza and large rotunda restaurant, it's a good place for a break, if you have time (from here to Corralejo will take an hour at most). After 8km (5 miles) or so, turn left onto the FV30, then right onto the FV207. After around 15km (9 miles), there is a fork in the road. Make sure you take the left one (the right one goes to Puerto del Rosario) which takes you back to Corralejo, via La Oliva.

# ① Corralejo

The biggest resort on the island, Corralejo divides neatly into old port and new resort, the dividing line being the pedestrianised zone next to the original fishing harbour, now the busy port.

The old part of town is a picturesque area of small alleys and squares, most of which lead onto a seafront promenade lined with attractive restaurants and bars. The centre is Music Square, as it is unofficially known, a tiny quadrangle hemmed in by restaurants, quiet by day but bustling by night. The best Spanish and local bars and restaurants, and some quaint little shops, are a block or two further on towards the port.

**Corralejo is a mix of modern resort and old port**

The modern part of town, also known as "The Strip", lies to either side of the Avenida Nuestra Señora del Carmen, and has basic shopping centres, amusement centres, cheap shops and eating places. At the top of the Avenida is Baku, which began life as a waterpark, with eight flumes and slides, rides and a swimming pool. It has now grown to include two other attractions – Animal Experience, with a petting zoo, sea lion and parrot shows, and El Hotel del Terror, a haunted house. Other family-orientated activities include an enchanted castle, a zipwire, paintballing, rock climbing and ten-pin bowling.

## Beaches

At the town harbour beach you can often admire some very sophisticated sand sculptures. Heading east, a narrow beach runs almost all the way along the front. The best beaches start about 500m (550 yards) east of here with glorious soft golden sands stretching for around 7km (4 miles), the only blot on

the landscape being two large hotels. Just before these is Flag Beach, home to windsurfers and kiteboarders. Whichever beach you choose, you will enjoy great views of Isla de Lobos and Lanzarote.

## Parque Natural de Las Dunas

On the other side of the road from the beaches, Corralejo's white sand dunes cover an area of around 27sq km (10 square miles). This area was declared a national park in 1982, too late to stop the two hotels that were already built here, but it has prevented further attempts to scar this otherwise pristine landscape. Walk for ten minutes off the road and you are in a Lawrence-of-Arabia desert world.

**Corralejo harbour**

### TAKING A BREAK

► 131–132 for some of the town's best options.

✚ 167 E5

**Baku**

✉ Avenida Nuestra Señora del Carmen ☎ 928 867 227, www.bakufuerteventura.com ◉ Daily 10–5 (later Jul, Aug, Sep) 💰 €20 adults, €13.50 children

---

### CORRALEJO: INSIDE INFO

**Top tips** Come over for the day during the second weekend in November and see the **Kite Festival** held by the dunes. It's a riot of colour.
• **Isla de Lobos** makes a wonderful day trip with a great beach, waymarked trails and fabulous views from its old volcano. Don't go on a windy day, however, as you will be sandblasted.

**Hidden gem** On Avenida Fuerteventura (the main road to the beaches) look out for the **Villa Tabaiba Galería de Arte** (next to an apartment complex with an Irish pub). Opening times are irregular but it's always worth stopping to peer into the garden to view this eccentric collection of Salvador Dalí- and Joan Miró-influenced artworks.

# 2 Betancuria

Once the island capital, Betancuria retains a real sense of history and several of its houses have original facades and doorways dating from the 16th and 17th centuries. It also has some of the best places to eat and drink on the island.

The island conqueror, Jean de Béthencourt, founded his capital here in 1404, well away from the coast, with the intention of avoiding Berber pirate attacks. Unfortunately, the raiders were undeterred and in 1593 they destroyed the church and took 600 islanders as slaves. The village remained the capital until 1834 but thereafter became a sleepy backwater until tourism gave it a fresh lease of life.

Betancuria maintains its traditions and sense of history

## Iglesia de Santa María

Rebuilt in 1620, this is the most beautiful church on the island, with naïve-style pastel-painted side altars, a baroque high altar, Gothic arches, wine-glass pulpit, *mudéjar*-influenced (Moorish) ceiling, and a graphic Judgement Day painting. It is no longer used for services.

## Casa Santa María

Located opposite the church, there is much more to the Casa Santa María than its restaurant and café (➤ 132). This is just a part of the largest house in the village, much of it dating from the 16th century, restored to become an island showcase, the Museo Artesanía. Here, beautifully arranged in a series of colonial wooden and stone rooms, terraces and courtyards, you will find island

merchandise for sale, tasting areas, an island audio-visual show, a video and exhibition of rural bygones, artisans at work, a cactus garden and a beautiful café.

## Museo de Arte Sacro

This small collection of religious art is housed in the 16th-century former residence of the church authorities.

### TAKING A BREAK

► 132 for the several options in and around Betancuria.

✚ 167 D3

Santa Maria Church

**Iglesia de Santa Maria**
✉ Museo de Arte Sacro Calle Carmelo Silvera ☎ 928 878 003 ◑ Mon–Fri 11–4:30, Sat 11–3:30
💷 Inexpensive (combined ticket for church and museum)

**Casa Santa María Museo Artesanía (Multivision, crafts and shops)**
✉ Plaza Iglesia ☎ 928 878 282
◑ Mon–Sat 11–4 💷 Expensive

---

### BETANCURIA: INSIDE INFO

**Top tips** The picture-postcard view of Betancuria is from the south on the main road. From here you get a **wonderful panorama**, across the dry riverbed, of the Iglesia de Santa María, surrounded by a cluster of venerable whitewashed buildings, and a green splash of palm trees.

**Must see** The Multivision **audio-visual show** at the Casa Santa María.

**One to miss** The uninspiring collection of **Guanche relics** in the Museo Arqueológico y Etnográfico.

**Hidden gems** The **bronze cannon** in front of the Museo Arqueológico was seized in 1740 from a troop of English privateers who were attacking the island. They were seen off by a group of 37 locals with muskets and agricultural tools. Thirty Englishmen and five locals were killed in the fighting. Set 200m (220 yards) north of the church in a gully just off the main road is the roofless ruin of the **Convento de San Buenaventura**. This Franciscan abbey was founded by monks who came over with the Norman conquerors.

# At Your Leisure

## 3 La Oliva

La Oliva is no more than a large
village but it has a number of notable
buildings. It is most famous for its
grandiose Casa de los Coroneles
(House of the Colonels), a large,
castellated, colonial-style house
dating back to 1650, home to the
island governors from 1709 to 1859
and recently reopened as an arts and
cultural centre (open Tue–Sat 10–6).
Another impressive structure is the
Iglesia de Nuestra Señora de la
Candelaria, built in 1711, with a
striking black lava-stone bell tower.
Its interior is very attractive with
features similar to the church at
Betancuria (➤ 127).

The Centro de Arte Canario
(CAC) is a cool contemporary space
devoted to Canarian art, complete
with soothing New Age music, and is
the type of art gallery that appeals to
most tastes.

➕ 167 E4

**Centro de Arte Canario**
✉ Calle Salvador Manrique de Lara
(opposite Casa de los Coronels)
☎ 928 868 233 🕐 Mon–Sat
10:30–2 💶 Moderate

## 4 Ecomuseo de La Alcogida

This open-air museum, set in typical
empty red-dust countryside, shows
rural life as it was some 50 to 100
years ago.

There are five houses and farms to
visit, and a hand-held audio device
gives a commentary in English or
German. Allow around an hour to
see everything.

The houses range from a simply-
furnished, modest house to a
well-to-do family house, a farm
with a working donkey-powered mill,
the miller's house and craftwork
demonstrations.

➕ 167 E4 ☎ 928 878 049 🕐 Tue–Fri,
Sun 9:30–5:30 💶 Moderate

Centro de Arte Canario for the best in
local art

## 5 Antigua

Like its close neighbour, Betancuria,
this old (*antigua*) village was
established in 1485 by settlers from
Normandy and Andalucía, and it too
was the capital of the island at one
time, although today, Antigua is
little more than a well-kept village.
In its pretty main square is the
diminutive white church of Nuestra
Señora de Antigua, built in 1785.
The interior is worth seeing.

Just north of the village is the Centro de Artesanía Molino, a mini-village museum and exhibition centre, constructed under the supervision of César Manrique. The centrepiece is a beautifully restored 200-year-old windmill set in a cactus garden. Its restaurant, housed in a large circular reconstructed wood-and-stone granary (► 132), is worth a look.

🔲 167 D3

**Centro de Artesanía Molino**
✉ In village centre ☎ 928 851 400
🕐 Tue–Fri, Sun 9:30–5 💷 Inexpensive

## ❻ La Lajita Oasis Park

It's a long way south (145km/90 miles from Corralejo) but you can spend most of the day here at Fuerteventura's biggest, best and longest-running tourist attraction. It has two good restaurants, and if you like animals and nature then it's worth a visit.

Oasis Park was established in 1985 as a garden centre, and even today first impressions are less of a zoo than of an oasis of vivid greenery (don't miss the splendid cactus garden) and vibrant-coloured plants set in the middle of a dusty desert.

One of the best features is the setting of enclosures, along narrow shady tracks with dense foliage, brightly coloured plants and running water. There are hundreds of reptiles, primates and mammals and birds, the sea lion, parrot and crocodile shows are fun for children and the birds of prey show is entertaining and informative.

Camel breeding is a speciality of the park and the herd is the largest in the Canaries at 220 strong. You can take camel rides (separate charge, expensive), and a visit to see the baby camels is recommended.

The African Savannah area has giraffes, antelopes and endangered African animals including rhinoceroses, though no predators.

🔲 166 C2 ✉ Carretera General de Jandía (FV2 km 57.4), La Lajita ☎ 902 400 434, www.lajitaoasispark.com
🕐 Daily 9–6 💷 Expensive

**Off the beaten track**
Just past the Ecomuseo de La Alcogida take the turning right onto the FV221 and drive 11km (7 miles) to the pretty little port of Los Molinos where there are two good seaside restaurants.

**Good places for kids**
• La Lajita Oasis Park (► left)
• Baku, Corralejo (► 125)

Camel rides around La Lajita Oasis Park are popular

# Where to...
# Eat and Drink

## Prices
Expect to pay for a three-course meal for one, excluding drinks and service
**€** under €15   **€€** €15–25   **€€€** €26–30   **€€€€** over €30

## CORRALEJO

### Ambaradam €
Set on a quiet side street, just off the top end of "The Strip", this Italian-owned and run café is a stylish, relaxed oasis in this part of town, perfect for a snack or full meal after visiting the market or the Baku amusement park. They specialise in breakfasts, sweet and savoury pancakes (no less than 47 kinds) and serve up to 14 different types of bruschetta. Attentive friendly young staff, good music, Italian football on TV.

➕ 167 E5 ☎ 696 996 207
📍 Calle Commercial Cactus
🕐 Mon–Sat 8am–1.30am

### Antiguo Café del Puerto €€
This is the sort of place where you will be made welcome at any time of the day or night, whether you want to drink a *café con leche* or a beer while watching the boats on the seafront, or to put together a meal from a good choice of tasty tapas in its attractive, pastel-washed, typically Spanish dining room. The staff are friendly and obliging.

➕ 167 E5 ☒ Calle La Ballena
☎ 928 535 844 🕐 Thu–Tue
11am–1am

### Café Latino €–€€
Set right on the front row of the promenade, with tables in a striking black pumice cactus garden, Café Latino is popular at most times of the day. International snacks make up much of the menu but there are tapas and interesting local dishes such as avocado, cheese and palm honey. If you want to eat, try to choose a quiet time, as service can be slow.

➕ 167 E5 ☒ Avenida Marítima 11
🕐 Daily 9pm–late

### Factoría €€€
Set right on the seafront, but just away from the main hubbub, this little pizzeria is one of the friendliest places in Corralejo. They do serve steaks and fish but specialise in pizzas (try something different such as the *felippini* with broccoli, bacon and salmon). The perfect dining choice for young families.

➕ 167 E5 ☒ Avenida Marítima
☎ 928 535 726
🕐 Daily 10:30am–11pm

### La Olá €
This attractive modern café attached to a bakery is just a stone's throw from the port. They do excellent breakfasts – try the *desayuno español* (Spanish breakfast), which includes toasted bread drizzled in olive oil, rubbed with tomato and topped with *jamón serrano* (cured ham). Despite being locals, they specialise in German pastries, cakes and cheesecake, and their iced coffee *frappé* is delicious. The service is friendly and fast, and there are comfy cane chairs; sit inside or out.

➕ 163 E5 ☒ Paseo Marítimo Bristol,
Muelle Grande ☎ 928 535 304
🕐 Wed–Mon 7:30am–8pm

## VILLAVERDE

### El Horno €€
The large barbecue at the entrance to this attractive rustic restaurant – decked in green gingham tablecloths and farming bygones – tells you that the speciality of the

house is grilled meats. Start with aubergine with cheese and palm honey then perhaps *cochinillo* (suckling pig) or kid. Finish with fig or *gofio* ice cream.

**⊞ 167 E4 ⊠ Carretera General Villaverde-La Oliva 191 (on the main road) ☎ 928 868 671, 629 382 304 ⏲ Tue–Sat 12:30–11, Sun 12:30–4.30**

### Hotel Rural Mahoh €€

Choose from one of the most interesting Canarian menus on the island while relaxing in one of its most charming settings. Start with croquettes, stuffed peppers or baby squid with *mojo verde*; for mains try *vieja* (parrotfish) or goat, and finish with *leche frita* or fig ice cream. The daily *menú de la casa* is excellent value, and on Sundays there are several roasts on the blackboard.

**⊞ 167 E4 ⊠ Sitio de Juan Bello, Carretera Villaverde-La Oliva (on the main road) ☎ 928 868 050, www.mahoh.com ⏲ Daily 1pm–midnight**

### BETANCURIA

### Casa Santa María €€–€€€€

The Casa Santa María café is entered through a dark, atmospheric bar hung with hams, garlic and huge cowbells. It sells home-made wines and moscatel from Lanzarote from the barrel. Two lovely sunny courtyards lead off here, and the main restaurant occupies a beautifully restored 16th-century colonial farmhouse. Antiques abound though they don't overpower, and the food is first class, albeit expensive (they do offer a daily set menu at a reasonable price).

There is also a café within the Museo Artesanía (separate entrance and admission charge, €€), which has an exquisite garden setting and serves excellent snacks and cakes.

**⊞ 167 E3 ⊠ Plaza de Santa María ☎ 928 878 282 ⏲ Main café and restaurant Sep–Jun 11–6, Jul–Aug 12–7. Museo Artesanía café Mon–Sat 11–4**

### Val Tarajal €€

This traditional dark-wood restaurant has few frills except for a giant 4m-long (13-foot) *timple* (a Canarian ukulele-like instrument) on one wall. All the usual Canarian favourites are on the menu, though some, like *puchero* and *sancocho*, are only available on Sundays and public holidays.

**⊞ 167 E3 ⊠ Calle Roberto Roldán 6 (main road) ☎ 928 878 007 ⏲ Tue–Sun 11–5**

### ANTIGUA

### La Molina €€

It feels almost as if you are stepping inside a huge windmill as you enter this large round building. In fact it used to be a granary. It has been beautifully restored with gleaming woodwork and inset lava stones forming brown-and-white giraffe-like patterns on the bare stone walls. Canarian music and rustic candelabras of inverted clay pots riddled with holes through which the light shines complete an atmospheric setting. The food is upmarket traditional island cuisine. Start with fried cheese with *mojo verde* or carpaccio of tuna. Then try goat stew or *cazuela de pescadores*, a special fish stew. This is popular with tour groups.

**⊞ 167 E3 ⊠ Carretera de Antigua, km20 (main road) ☎ 928 878 577 ⏲ Tue–Fri, Sun 10–6, meals 12–3**

### VEGA DE RIO PALMAS

### Don Antonio €€€€

Set 3km (2 miles) south of Betancuria, this German-owned gourmet restaurant is housed in a very pretty lilac-trimmed colonial house. It is possibly the most expensive restaurant on the island, but the food and surroundings are unbeatable.

**⊞ 167 E3 ⊠ Plaza Iglesia ☎ 928 878 757 ⏲ Tue–Sun 10–5**

# Walks and Drives

# 1 ARRECIFE
*Walk*

This easy walk, much of it by the water, takes in all aspects of the capital: shopping, history, architecture, culture and its role as a port. If you haven't been here for a few years you will be amazed at how visitor-friendly it has become.

**Much of this walk is along the waterfront**

**DISTANCE** 4km (2.5 miles) **TIME** 1 hr 30 mins–2 hrs
**START POINT** Gran Hotel **END POINT** Castillo de San José (alternative circular walk ending in the town centre at Calle de León y Castillo) ✚ 163 D2

Note: you may wish to reverse the direction of this walk. Both the Gran Hotel and the Castillo de San José have recommended restaurants open for lunch.

## 1–2

There's no missing the Gran Hotel. Whatever you think about it, this striking, redesigned 17-storey hotel with a chequered history (▶ 92) is the bold new face of the city and around it there is a considerable amount of work going on. The man-made beach of Playa del Reducto has been smartened up with an attractive facelift and landscaping is in progress at the other end of the beach. A new nightclub and government buildings are in place

and this whole area is poised to become a focal point for locals and increasingly, foreign visitors too. Take the lift to the top to enjoy the views.

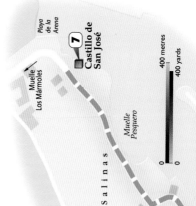

*Playa de la Arena*

*Muelle Los Mármoles*

*Muelle Pesquero*

S a l i n a s

**7** **Castillo de San José**

Polígono Industrial

0    400 metres
0    400 yards

## 2–3

Turn right out of the hotel and walk along the front. Go around the corner, by the Yacht Club and onto the smart tiled promenade of the Avenida La Marina (formerly Avenida Generalissimo Franco) with its beautiful tropical gardens and sculptures. The building at the start of the promenade is the Open University. In front of it stands a statue of the physicist Don Blas Cabrera Felipe (1878–1945), "a favourite son of the city" whom you can learn more about at the Casa de los Arroyos (▶ 137).

The Avenida boasts a number of different architectural styles. At No 14 is a white neo-classical house dated 1917, and next door is a lovely 19th-century house with a traditional wooden Canarian balcony. Just past the Correos (post office) and opposite the restored gleaming wooden bandstand (home to the tourist office) is the 19th-century Casa de la Cultura Agustín de la Hoz. The town hall until the early 1980s, it is now an exhibition and concert space.

**Taking a Break**
The kiosk on the front almost opposite the entrance to the Castillo de San Gabriel (▶ 83) is a good spot for a coffee.

**Enjoy the modern art at the Castillo de San José**

Isla de Cruces

Escuelas de Náutica y Pesca (6)

Hospital Insular

Puerto de Naos

CALLE JUAN DE QUESADA

Hiper Dino/ C C Atlántico (5)

Charco de San Ginés

AVENIDA DE SAN MANRIQUE

CALLE DE LEÓN Y CASTILLO

Iglesia de San Ginés

CALLE LIEBRE

Mercado

Casa de los Arroyos

Isla del Francés

CALLE DE LEÓN Y CASTILLO (4)

CALLE JOSÉ ANTONIO PRIMO RIVERA

CALLE DE LEÓN Y CASTILLO

Casa de la Cultura Agustín de la Hoz (3)

AVENIDA DE LA MARINA

Castillo de San Gabriel

Islote de San Gabriel

AV DE RAFAEL GLEZ NEGRÍN

Gran Hotel (1)

(2)

Islote de Fermina

Playa del Reducto

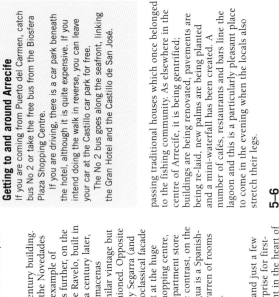

## Getting to and around Arrecife

If you are coming from Puerto del Carmen, catch bus No 2 or take the free bus from the Biosfera Plaza Shopping Centre.

If you are driving, there is a car park beneath the hotel, although it is quite expensive. If you intend doing the walk in reverse, you can leave your car at the Castillo car park for free.

The No 2 bus goes along the seafront, linking the Gran Hotel and the Castillo de San José.

passing traditional houses which once belonged to the fishing community. As elsewhere in the centre of Arrecife, it is being gentrified; buildings are being renovated, pavements are being re-laid, new palms are being planted and a mini-waterfall has been created. A number of cafés, restaurants and bars line the lagoon and this is a particularly pleasant place to come in the evening when the locals also stretch their legs.

### 5–6

Turn left at the end of the lagoon into Calle Juan de Quesada. After 250m (270 yards), set back on the left-hand side, is the Hospital Insular (Island

see another typical early 20th-century building. Above the fashion shop Planet, the Novedades Vashi building is an interesting example of 1970s architecture. A few metres further, on the right, it is interesting to compare Ravelo, built in 1894 and beautifully renovated a century later, with its next-door neighbour Almacenas Arencibia, which is of a very similar vintage but has remained resolutely old-fashioned. Opposite here, the building now owned by Segarra (and others) is a faded white-tiled neoclassical facade dated 1914. The shops peter out at the huge modern Hiper Dino/Atlantico shopping centre, which houses a supermarket, department store and cinema. By way of complete contrast, on the other side of the street, Tamaragua is a Spanish-Colonial-style property with a warren of rooms built around a central courtyard.

### 4–5

Turn right past the Hiper Dino and just a few metres away there is quite a surprise for first-time visitors to the capital. Right in the heart of the city is a large and very peaceful lagoon, the Charco de San Ginés, a welcome break from the shopping bustle. Go left and skirt it clockwise

### 3–4

Turn left into the pedestrianised Calle de León y Castillo. As on the seafront, you will find an interesting mix of architectural styles. Note the old building on the first right-hand corner (the lower floor is occupied by Mango) with its traditional wooden balconies and stone-framed windows. Next to it the tile-fronted Cabildo Insular (Island Government) headquarters dates from 1900. Further along on the left wander inside the shop now owned by Tomas Panasco to

Hospital). In front is a garden of mature trees. Note the unusual abstract lava rock sculpture, which incorporates a ship's windlass and is similar to that in the gardens on the promenade. It is by César Manrique, dated 1968, and is dedicated to Don José Molina, a prominent doctor at the hospital, who died in 1966.

Opposite is the Instituto Marítimo Pesquero de Canarias (Canary Fishing Institute), which incorporates the Escuelas de Náutica y Pesca (College of Fishing). Here, young men come from all over Spain to study the latest techniques of seafaring and deep-sea fishing. The College's tapas bar is open to the public and if anyone knows fresh fish these guys do.

### 6–7

Continue walking along the seafront, and in the Muelle Pesquero (Fishing Harbour) you will see the largest Canarian commercial fishing fleet in the archipelago. (The fleet at Las Palmas, Gran Canaria, is slightly larger but is boosted by Spanish and African boats). The Lanzarote fleet is also the oldest in the Canaries, dating back to the 14th and 15th centuries when, it is said, they built their boats after the styles of pirate ships, which frequently raided this coast. Unfortunately these are difficult times for the fleet as international directives have stopped

them from harvesting their traditional Mauritanian fishing grounds. The imperative is therefore to replace lost revenue with leisure craft and a marina.

Continue on, and the area you see to your left with the small windmills was once a saltpan.

At the end of the port stands the 18th-century Castillo de San José, brilliantly restored by César Manrique to become home to a world-class collection of modern art. It also houses one of the island's top restaurants (▶ 85 and 90). Opposite here the deep-sea port of Muelle Los Mármoles welcomes cruise ships.

### A shorter alternative circular walk

At point 5, turn right instead of left and head back towards the town centre along the seafront. Take a look in the fish market (*mercado*) at the junction with Calle Liebre. It's small and modern but there are often some colourful specimens in here. Go up Calle Liebre and turn left. The parish church of San Ginés (▶ 84) stands in a charming square ahead of you. Turn left out of the square back to the seafront, then right and you will come to the Casa de los Arroyos, a beautiful colonial house (▶ 84) which you can enter. The pedestrianised Calle de Leon y Castillo is just a few metres away on your right.

**The castle restaurant has great views across the harbour**

### Best time to visit

Wednesday morning when the craft market is in progress on the promenade. Avoid Sunday when the shops are closed. Morning is the best time so you can catch the shops before they close for siesta and you finish the walk just in time for lunch.

## 2 TEGUISE
*Walk*

Teguise is a perfect town for a walking tour, with history and character oozing from the fabric of most of its perfectly preserved buildings, which are protected by planning controls. It is small, easy to navigate and mostly traffic free.

Visit the 18th-century Palacio Spinola

**DISTANCE** approx 2km (1 mile) **TIME** 1 hour 30 mins
**START/END POINT** Plaza San Miguel ⊞ 163 D4

### 1–2

The landmark church of Nuestra Señora de Guadalupe is the logical place to begin a tour of this historic town. Although the church originally dates from 1420 it has been rebuilt many times. It suffered severe fire damage in 1909 and was unsympathetically restored.

From the church walk to the opposite side of the square (Plaza San Miguel) to Caja

Canarias, formerly La Cilla, a sturdy stone house dating from 1680. In medieval times one-tenth of all the crops grown on Lanzarote were given to the church and it was stored here. Opposite the church is the Palacio Spinola, built between 1730 and 1780 (▶ 56), now property of the Teguise Town Council, acting as tourist office, museum and official residence of the Canary Islands Government.

Directly opposite here, the 18th-century building next to the church is the Teguise campus of the University of Las Palmas.

On the lower corner of the square is the Policía Municipal, once the house

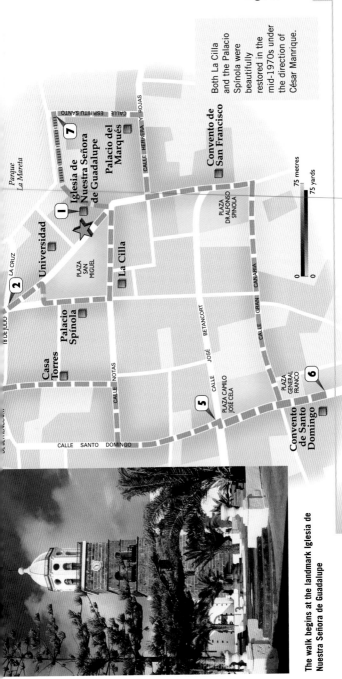

Both La Cilla and the Palacio Spinola were beautifully restored in the mid-1970s under the direction of César Manrique.

**The walk begins at the landmark Iglesia de Nuestra Señora de Guadalupe**

the 18th century and is the Casa Cuartel (Barracks) de la Guardia Civil (the state police force). In front of it, turn right along Calle Puerto y Villa de Garachico, then left into Plaza Reina Ico. Note the typical red-painted stone doorway at No 2. Straight ahead is the simple chapel of the Ermita de la Vera Cruz, founded in 1841. It holds paintings and objects which came from Portugal in the 17th century. Unfortunately

has been superbly restored by the current owners and doubles as an art gallery and restaurant (➤ 69).

Next door, La Bodeguita del Medio once functioned as a mortuary, very different from its current function as a lively tapas bar (➤ 68). Its neighbour, Galería La Ville, is one of the few old houses in the town to have retained its central patio area. You can go right inside, past the Moroccan shop that now occupies the front.

With your back to Ikarus, the large house on the right-hand side of the Plaza 18 de Julio is now a carpet shop but originally housed the town's first hospital (Hospital del Espíritu Santo), established in 1473. The current building dates from the early 18th century.

## 3–4

In the next square, the typical Canarian house, painted white with a balcony (the only one of its kind in Teguise), was built in

**Cheese and wine make tasty souvenirs**

## Place names

Plaza Maciot de Béthencourt takes its name from the nephew and successor to the island conqueror, Jean de Béthencourt. It was Maciot who founded Teguise in 1418, naming it (according to legend) after his bride, Princess Teguise, the daughter of the Guanche king Guadarfía.

of a prominent local citizen in the mid-17th century. Pick up a free town map from here. The house now occupied by the Malvasía shop, opposite, is of a similar age.

Look out for the wooden cross next to Malvasía: there are 14 of these dotted around the town marking the Stations of the Cross, used in the Semana Santa (Holy Week) procession at Easter time.

## 2–3

Enter the beautiful square of Plaza 18 de Julio and see the statue of a lady carrying a pitcher of water. On the right-hand side of the square (which becomes Plaza Clavijo y Fajardo), examine the handsome row of buildings. The one occupied by Ikarus is about 250 years old and was the home of the Justice of the Peace. It it is rarely open to the public, though you may be able to get a key if you ask next door at the Escuela de Artesanía (Artisan's School). Here local craftspeople learn their skills, and if you are lucky you may get to see them making the island's characteristic instrument, the *timple*.

### 4–5

Take Calle Dr Alfred Spinola, opposite the Escuela de Artesanía, turn left into Calle el Rayo (back towards the Casa Cuartel), then first right into Calle Carnicería, the street which once housed the town's butchers, now devoid of shops.

On the right-hand side are the town archives, the Archivo Histórico, set in an 18th-century building. If you speak a little Spanish they will be only too pleased to answer any queries you may have about the town's history.

Turn into Calle Correo, opposite the Archivo Histórico, and cross Plaza Maciot de Bethencourt into Calle Higuera. On the right-hand side, look into the Tierra shop to see how they have beautifully restored this 19th-century building.

On the opposite side, a little further along, is the Casa Torres, a splendid 18th-century house with wooden shutters with carved panels. At the end of this street turn right into Calle Notas to find a charming little 1930s-style red-and-white former cinema. Today it is occupied by Emporium Antiques. On the corner just past here, turn left into Calle Santo Domingo and use the zebra crossing to get over the busy main Yaiza road.

### 5–6

The large square of Plaza Camilo José Cela has a grand entrance arch, and the building on the far side of the square is the Casa Spinola, another property owned by the town's wealthiest family. It once belonged to the Dominican Order whose

Take a peek inside **Nuestra Señora de Guadalupe**

former monastery is just across the street. On the right-hand side of the street take a break at the rustic Café Tahona with its pretty internal patio. Opposite here is the Casa de Castillo, a beautiful house now home to Indigo clothes boutique.

Cross back over to the handsome Convento de Santo Domingo (▶ 57) built in the 17th century. It is now used as a modern art gallery. The building next door is now the town hall. Have a look inside and you will see it has retained the original cloister arcade.

### 6–7

Retrace your steps and turn right past Indigo into Calle Gran Canaria. Directly ahead, the Castillo de Santa Bárbara (▶ 57) sits high on the hill in the distance. Calle Gran Canaria ends at the Convento de San Francisco, now home to the Museo de Arte Sacro (▶ 57). Continue left past the church and turn right into Calle Marqués de Herrera y Rojas. The Palacio del Marques, on the left, is the oldest house in Teguise and it has an exquisite garden

which is now the Patio del Vino, open for refreshments (▶ 57 and 69). To the right, on the other side of Calle Espíritu Santo, its neighbour is the municpal theatre or Teatrillo ("Little Theatre"). It occupies the nave of the old church of Espíritu Santo, which was built in 1730, and has been a theatre since 1825.

Calle Espíritu Santo leads to the Parque La Mareta, a wide, open space that is the centrepiece of the Sunday market. It was formerly a giant cistern, or mini reservoir, and provided the city's drinking water.

### 7–1

Turn left, take the steps and turn left again into Calle La Sangre at the rear of the church. It takes its name (Street of Blood) from the 16th century when pirate raids were frequent, and in 1586 many townsfolk were slaughtered here. Keep to the right and you are back in the Plaza San Miguel in front of the church.

Every Sunday there's a market in Parque La Mareta

# NORTH
## 3 Drive

**DISTANCE** 58km (36 miles) **TIME** 2–3 hours
**START/END POINT** Tahiche (Fundación César Manrique roundabout) ✚ 163 D3

This full-day drive will show you the best of north and central Lanzarote. The roads are fast and straight in the north, often slow and tortuous in the heart of the island, but well worth the effort, with magnificent mountain scenery.

This tour of the north shows that Lanzarote has much more in the way of spectacular scenery that just its Fire Mountains. The north is also indelibly stamped by the hand of the great Lanzarote artist César Manrique, and if you haven't already got the lowdown on him then it's a good idea to visit the Fundación César Manrique (▶ 54–55) right at the start of the tour. This would make it a long day out, so if you can do it on another occasion it may be better.

### 1–2

The roundabout we begin from is marked by a huge silver wind mobile, designed by César Manrique, of course! Head north on the LZ10

towards Teguise. Tahiche and neighbouring Nazaret are two of the island's more fashionable places to live, as you can see from some of the properties just off the roadside. Continue on to Teguise with excellent views of the countryside falling away to the west (on your left). Ahead of you to the right, high above Teguise, stands the Castillo de Santa Bárbara (▶ 57). You won't have time to visit Teguise on this itinerary, but if you want a coffee pop into the Restaurant Suso, on the main road opposite the entrance to the town.

Continue on the LZ10 which begins to climb and wind. Los Valles is a very well tended pretty little village. It sits on the edge of a basin and the fields are cultivated into large squares, giving a very neat and geometric feel to the whole landscape. Traditional low houses with small windows, women in the fields wearing traditional bonnets (▶ 146) to keep out wind

**Traditionally cactuses were grown for breeding the cochineal beetle**

**Best time to visit**

Avoid Sunday when the Teguise market means the roads around here will be busy. Go on Saturday to visit the Haría craft market.

and dust, and old men wearing black felt hats or cloth trilbies complete a very rural bygone scene. You can take it all in from the Mirador de los Valles, signposted off to the right where there is also a good restaurant that serves breakfasts.

### 2–3

Continue for another 3km (2 miles) or so, and as the giant golf ball, which marks the tracking station for Peñas del Chache (ahead to your left), gets ever closer, there is a turn-off on the other side of the road, marked Parque Eólico. Here you will find the huge wind turbines that you may have seen from elsewhere on the island. There's nothing else at this park apart from landscaped gardens, but the views, all the way down to Arrecife, are excellent. For great views of the opposite coast turn off left after another 1km (0.5 miles) to the Ermita de Las Nieves (Hermitage of the Snows). Snow is unlikely but

it may be blowing a gale so wrap up well. Below lies the beach of Famara (▶ 64), with the regular shaped roofs of its Bungalows Famara holiday homes creating quite a striking pattern. To the right looms the Risco de Famara (Famara cliffs) and beyond are

Lanzarote's northern islands.

The military installations at Peñas del Chache are out of bounds, which is a shame as this occupies the island's highest point at 672m (2,204 feet).

Return to the main road.

**Admire the traditional architecture in the villages en route**

### 3–4

From here it's downhill all the way to Haría, and it is a spectacular descent with two *miradores* (lookout points) along the way. The first is Los Helechos, too far away to get a really good view of

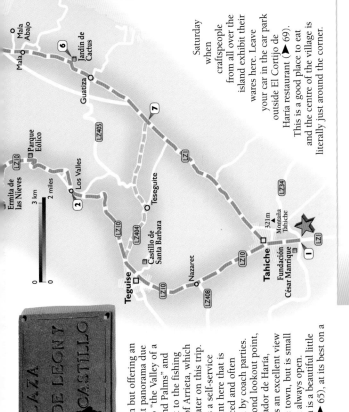

The mighty Monte Corona dominates inland views

the town but offering an excellent panorama due north to "the Valley of a Thousand Palms" and due east to the fishing village of Arrieta, which comes later on this trip. There is a self-service restaurant here that is overpriced and often overrun by coach parties. The second lookout point, the Mirador de Haría, provides an excellent view into the town, but is small and not always open.

Haría is a beautiful little town (▶ 65), at its best on a

Saturday when craftspeople from all over the island exhibit their wares here. Leave your car in the car park outside El Cortijo de Haría restaurant (▶ 69). This is a good place to eat and the centre of the village is literally just around the corner.

## 4–5

Continue through the narrow streets of the village, following the signs towards the Mirador del Río and passing through the neat little village of Máguez. If you think you have already seen enough *miradores* for one day, think again, as this is the mother of all *miradores* and a truly brilliant creation by César Manrique (▶ 10–12). Return to the main road and begin heading south. The landscape is now dominated by the mighty broken-coned Monte Corona, at 605m (1,985 feet) the tallest volcano on the island. Its debris, the Malpaís de la Corona, covers this whole northwest corner

**Haría is best visited on Saturday when local craftspeople bring out their wares**

of the island and beneath it lie two of the island's finest tourist attractions, Jameos del Agua (▶ 59–61) and the Cueva de los Verdes (▶ 62).

Shortly after returning to the main road, look on your right for handwritten signs to the Bodega Volcán Corona. This is a very rustic place and worth a visit for location and atmosphere, as well as to sample its wine. As you descend the slopes of the mountain you will see field upon field of vines. The large white castellated building at the top of the hill is part

of the Bodega Volcán Corona. It looks rather sinister and the locals say it is haunted.

### 5–6

Continue your descent, which eventually meets the coast at Arrieta. Turn right at the roundabout marked by a red-cone César Manrique wind mobile if you want to visit one of the town's fish restaurants, otherwise stay on the main road (now the LZ1) heading towards Arrecife. After another 3km (2 miles) or so turn off left towards Mala and Guatiza. You will soon notice that the fields are covered with cacti and after another 2–3km (1–2 miles) you arrive at the world's most unusual cactus garden, the Jardín de Cactus (▶ 63). It's also a perfect refreshment stop.

### 6–1

This road rejoins the main road after another 2km (1 mile) and it is then 7km (4 miles) back to Tahiche where you turn left to get back to the start point of the excursion.

### 7

**Optional extension**

If you are in no hurry to return home, after rejoining the LZ1 south of the Jardín de Cactus, take the next turn right towards Teseguite,

Almost immediately to either side of the road you will come across strangely shaped rock formations with isolated columns or blocks the size of boats, perhaps with holes in where the soft rock has eroded. This is the combined effect of quarrying and wind erosion. Continue onto the village of Teseguite where you will find (on the right-hand side) one of the island's best and friendliest art galleries, Arte Cerámica. This road emerges onto the LZ10, just north of Teguise, so turn left here and enjoy a meal or a drink in one of the town's many excellent bars or restaurants (▶ 68–69). As you head south from Teguise you may also like to look in at the extraordinary LagOmar bar and restaurant complex (▶ 68)

### Sombreros and campesinas

The women working the fields (who are known as *campesinas*) often wear a cone-shaped straw hat tied with a ribbon, which is known as a *sombrero de la Graciosa* or a *sombrero de San Bartolomé*. The white cloth bonnet you may see is a sign that the woman wearing it is unmarried: this hat is known as a *sombrero de la campesina*. The man's trilby is known as a *chapeo* or *sombrero de campesino*.

# 4 SOUTH
### Drive

**DISTANCE** 57km (35 miles) **TIME** 2–3 hours
**START/END POINT** Mácher roundabout (LZ2) ⊞ 165 E3

This meandering drive through some of Lanzarote's most beautiful and timeless scenery will show you both natural and man-made wonders. The final leg, through the vineyards of La Geria, is quite extraordinary. Like its wines, this is a landscape to be savoured in a leisurely manner.

## 1–2

Drive west towards Yaiza for 7km (4 miles) with the mountains of the south looming before you and turn left at the roundabout towards Femés. Pass through the neat little hamlet of Las Casitas and note the very last house on the right-hand side. Astonishingly, in addition to its display of nautical paraphernalia, it also has a small US attack helicopter parked in its front garden. In winter the landscape around here is very green, and the fields are reminiscent of alpine meadows. The road continues to climb and reaches its zenith at the volcanic peak of

**Take a leisurely drive, passing beautiful villages such as Uga**

Atalaya de Femés at 609m 1,998 feet).

Sitting in a saddle of the mountain, the little village of Femés looks right down to Playa Blanca, the Isla de Lobos and Fuerteventura. The church here, the Ermita San Marcial del Rubicón, was founded in the 15th century and was one of the first on the island. It was destroyed in the 16th century by pirates, and the current church dates from 1733 (open only for weekend masses). San Marcial is the island patron saint and the Plain of El Rubicón lies below you. It was here that the island conqueror Jean de Béthencourt landed in the summer of

### Taking a break

If it's lunchtime you won't get a fresher meal of fish or seafood than at El Golfo (▶ 112), but you may prefer to wait until you get to Yaiza to eat in what is possibly the most famous restaurant on the island, La Era (▶ 112).

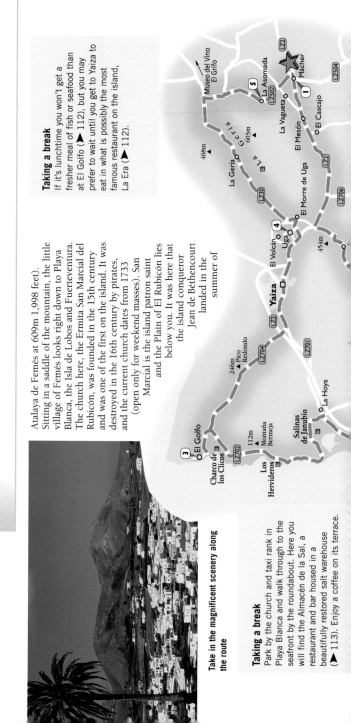

Take in the magnificent scenery along the route

### Taking a break

Park by the church and taxi rank in Playa Blanca and walk through to the seafront by the roundabout. Here you will find the Almacén de la Sal, a restaurant and bar housed in a beautifully restored salt warehouse (▶ 113). Enjoy a coffee on its terrace.

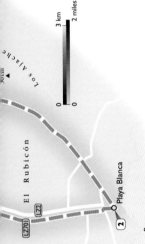

1402 and made a peace pact with the last of the island's Guanche kings, Guadarfía.

Continue down to Playa Blanca and stop for a coffee on the seafront.

**2–3**

Return north on the main road, but at the first roundabout, instead of taking the main LZ2 road, take the LZ701, which runs parallel to it. After 8km (5 miles) you can pull over to the left and enjoy the view over the Salinas de Janubio saltpans (▲ 110). Alternatively, wait until you have just passed the front of the saltpans and pull in on your left at the *mirador* restaurant where you can dine or have a drink right next to picture windows overlooking the saltpans. Keep on the same road and after 1.4km (1 mile) you come to a black sand beach (no swimming here) where beachcombers are often busy. They are looking for volcanic "bombs", which they then proceed to smash open in the hope of finding olivine.

Keep following the road around the shoreline, and take a break to explore the grottoes of Los Hervideros (▲ 110), particularly if it is a stormy

day. As you drive on past here the Montaña Bermeja (Purple Mountain) is a curious sight with its bright purples and orange hues, quite out of place in the almost monotone black landscape.

As you get closer to El Golfo a bizarre profile of jagged, torn rock looms directly ahead of you. Take the short detour left to follow the Charco de Los Clicos sign to see the striated rocks here and to enjoy the view of the beach from this angle. Return to your car and then drive round the corner, following the El Golfo sign to the village itself and the cliff path that gives the best view of its famous lagoon (▲ 110).

### View the island from a different perspective

**3–4**

Return the way you came, out of El Golfo, and continue straight ahead at the roundabout through the centre of Yaiza, one of Lanzarote's best-kept villages (▲ 111). Just as you are leaving the village and approaching the next roundabout look left to see the unusual pink facade of the Finca de las Salinas, one of the

The saltpans at Salinas de Janubio are reckoned to be the biggest salt producer in the archipelago

islands' best rural hotels (▲114). Just to the left of the roundabout a windmill has been truncated and converted to a learning centre by the island government. Go straight ahead on the LZ2 back towards Arrecife, with the village of Uga to your left. Like Yaiza, this is impeccably kept and also features a superb restaurant, the Bodega Uga (best in the evenings, ▲35). Uga is most famous for its very popular Ahumaderia (smokehouse) and shop, which provides much of the island with its smoked salmon (▲116). Take the turn left just after the shop onto the LZ30. This climbs and gives an excellent view, down to your left back to Uga. The large open circular area is its old *mareta* (reservoir/water cistern).

### 4–5

The LZ30 is Lanzarote's most picturesque and most memorable road, cutting through the heart of La Geria (▲107–108). Signs do warn drivers that the road is in *mal estado* (a bad state), but you'll soon realise that you wouldn't want it any other way. Not only is it completely in harmony with the landscape, you will be so transfixed by the views that you will be pleased you have to drive slowly. The road narrows in places to almost a single track, though passing points generally allow a smooth flow of traffic. To the left the mountains of Timanfaya

National Park provide an epic backdrop to the surreal black canvas of a thousand horseshoe-shaped vine shelters.

The first bodega is the Bodega La Geria, which is well worth a visit (▲108). Continue, and just 100m (110 yards) after this, look for a small track to the right with the sign of a knife and fork. This leads to Bodega El Chupadero, incorporating a charming little wine bar

(▲108). Back on the main road the next bodega is that of A Suarez, often frequented by coach tours. After another 2–3km (1–2 miles) turn right towards La Asomada, back onto a well-surfaced road.

### 5–1

Pass through La Asomada back to the Macher roundabout on the main LZ2 road

# Practicalities

## GETTING ADVANCE INFORMATION

### Websites
• www.turismolanzarote.com is the official site.
• www.lanzarote.com is a very good site.
Other sites worth a look are: www.discoverlanzarote.com, www.lanzaroteisland.com and www.gazettelanzarote.com, the website of *Lanzarote Gazette*, an English-language weekly magazine.

### In the UK
Spanish Tourist Office
79 New Cavendish Street
London W1W 6XB
☎ 020 7486 8077

## BEFORE YOU GO

### WHAT YOU NEED

| | | | | | | | | |
|---|---|---|---|---|---|---|---|---|
| ● Required | | | | | | | | |
| ○ Suggested | | | | | | | | |
| ▲ Not required | | | | | | | | |
| △ Not applicable | UK | Germany | USA | Canada | Australia | Ireland | Netherlands | Spain |
| Passport/National Identity Card | ● | ● | ● | ● | ● | ● | ● | ● |
| Visa | ▲ | ▲ | ▲ | ▲ | ▲ | ▲ | ▲ | ▲ |
| Onward or Return Ticket | ○ | ○ | ● | ● | ● | ○ | ○ | ○ |
| Health Inoculations (tetanus and polio) | ▲ | ▲ | ▲ | ▲ | ▲ | ▲ | ▲ | ▲ |
| Health Documentation (► 156) | ● | ● | ▲ | ▲ | ▲ | ● | ● | |
| Travel Insurance | ○ | ○ | ○ | ○ | ○ | ○ | ○ | ○ |
| Driver's Licence (national) | ● | ● | ● | ● | ● | ● | ● | ● |
| Car Insurance Certificate | ● | ● | ● | ● | ● | ● | ● | ● |
| Car Registration Document | ● | ● | ● | ● | ● | ● | ● | ○ |

### WHEN TO GO

**Lanzarote**

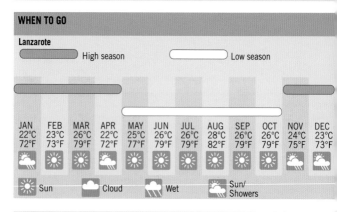

| | JAN | FEB | MAR | APR | MAY | JUN | JUL | AUG | SEP | OCT | NOV | DEC |
|---|---|---|---|---|---|---|---|---|---|---|---|---|
| | 22°C | 23°C | 26°C | 22°C | 25°C | 26°C | 26°C | 28°C | 26°C | 26°C | 24°C | 23°C |
| | 72°F | 73°F | 79°F | 72°F | 77°F | 79°F | 79°F | 82°F | 79°F | 79°F | 75°F | 73°F |

High season    Low season

☀ Sun    ☁ Cloud    🌧 Wet    ⛅ Sun/Showers

The temperatures above are the **average daily maximum** for each month. Minimum temperatures rarely drop below 15°C (59°F); a year-round spring climate means that average temperatures range from 19°C (66°F) in winter to 26°C (79°F) in summer. The sea temperature varies from 19°C (66°F) in January to 24°C (75°F) in September. Most of the rain falls in the north and there is occasional snow in the mountains. The north is also affected by the *mar de nubes* ("sea of clouds"), low-lying clouds brought by the trade winds, and the *panza de burro* ("donkey's belly"), a grey haze which produces intense heat in summer. There is a second peak in July and August, when many Spanish families are on holiday. The quietest months are May, June, September and October.

**In the USA**

Tourist Office of Spain
666 Fifth Ave (35th Floor)
New York NY 10103
☎ 212/265-8822

Tourist Office of Spain
1221 Brickell Ave
Miami FL 33131
☎ 305/358-1992

For a complete list
of Spanish tourist
offices abroad, see
www.tourspain.info.

## GETTING THERE

### By air

There are numerous charter flights throughout the year from London and other European cities. Most seats are sold by tour operators as part of a package holiday, but it is possible to buy a flight-only deal through travel agents on the internet. For independent travellers, the disadvantage of charter flights is that you are usually restricted to a period of either seven or 14 days.

The Spanish national airline, **Iberia**, operates regular scheduled flights to Lanzarote, but these are expensive and unless you are already in Spain they are not worth considering.

If you can get a cheap flight to Fuerteventura, but not Lanzarote, do so then take a ferry (▶ below) from Corralejo to Puerto del Carmen or Playa Blanca.

### Inter-island travel

**By air  Binter Canarias** (www.binternet.com) offer daily flights from Lanzarote to the other Canary Islands.

**By sea**  Regular ferry services to Corralejo (Fuerteventura) from Playa Blanca (▶ 40) **Fred Olsen**  operates the *Bocayna Express* catamaran (tel: 902 100 107, www.fredolsen.es); **Naviera Armas** operate the *Volcán de Tindaya* (tel: 902 456 500, www.navieraarmas.com); **Princess Ico/Motobarcos Arosa** operates the *Princesa Ico Fuerteventura Express* (tel: 928 514 322 or 629 731 293, www.princesa-ico.com). It also operates a service to Puerto del Carmen.

**Regular ferry services to other destinations Trasmediterránea** (www.trasmediterranea.es) and **Naviera Armas** (▶ above) operate from Arrecife to Puerto de Rosario on Fuerteventura and to Las Palmas on Gran Canaria. **Naviera Armas** also operate a service to the islands of Tenerife and La Palma. **Líneas Romero** operate from Orzola to La Graciosa (tel: 928 842 055, www.lineares-romeo.com).

## TIME

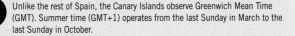

Unlike the rest of Spain, the Canary Islands observe Greenwich Mean Time (GMT). Summer time (GMT+1) operates from the last Sunday in March to the last Sunday in October.

## CURRENCY AND FOREIGN EXCHANGE

**Currency**  As in the rest of Spain, the Canary Islands have adopted the euro. Notes are in denominations of 5, 10, 20, 50, 100, 200, 500; coins come in 1, 2, 5, 10, 20 and 50 cents and 1 and 2 euros.

**Credit cards**  Major credit cards are widely accepted in the resorts, but don't rely on these elsewhere.

**Exchange**  Banks generally offer the best rates for changing foreign currency and traveller's cheques, though money can be exchanged at travel agents, hotels and exchange bureaux. When changing traveller's cheques you will need to show your passport. You can also withdraw cash from **ATM (cashpoint) machines** using your credit or debit card and PIN. The rate of exchange is often better than what you will get elsewhere, though your account holder will usually make a charge for this service.

# WHEN YOU ARE THERE

## CLOTHING SIZES

| UK | Rest of Europe | USA | |
|---|---|---|---|
| 36 | 46 | 36 | **Suits** |
| 38 | 48 | 38 | |
| 40 | 50 | 40 | |
| 42 | 52 | 42 | |
| 44 | 54 | 44 | |
| 46 | 56 | 46 | |
| 7 | 41 | 8 | **Shoes** |
| 7.5 | 42 | 8.5 | |
| 8.5 | 43 | 9.5 | |
| 9.5 | 44 | 10.5 | |
| 10.5 | 45 | 11.5 | |
| 11 | 46 | 12 | |
| 14.5 | 37 | 14.5 | **Shirts** |
| 15 | 38 | 15 | |
| 15.5 | 39/40 | 15.5 | |
| 16 | 41 | 16 | |
| 16.5 | 42 | 16.5 | |
| 17 | 43 | 17 | |
| 8 | 34 | 6 | **Dresses** |
| 10 | 36 | 8 | |
| 12 | 38 | 10 | |
| 14 | 40 | 12 | |
| 16 | 42 | 14 | |
| 18 | 44 | 16 | |
| 4.5 | 38 | 6 | **Shoes** |
| 5 | 38 | 6.5 | |
| 5.5 | 39 | 7 | |
| 6 | 39 | 7.5 | |
| 6.5 | 40 | 8 | |
| 7 | 41 | 8.5 | |

## NATIONAL HOLIDAYS

| 1 Jan | New Year's Day |
|---|---|
| 6 Jan | Epiphany |
| 2 Feb | Candlemas |
| 19 Mar | St Joseph's Day |
| Mar/Apr | Good Friday, Easter Monday |
| 1 May | Labour Day |
| 30 May | Canary Islands' Day |
| May/June | Corpus Christi |
| 25 July | St James's Day |
| 15 Aug | Assumption of the Virgin |
| 12 Oct | Columbus Day |
| 1 Nov | All Saints' Day |
| 6 Dec | Constitution Day |
| 8 Dec | Feast of the Immaculate Conception |
| 25 Dec | Christmas Day |

## OPENING HOURS

○ Shops ● Post offices
● Offices ○ Museums
● Banks ○ Pharmacies

8am 9am 10am noon 1pm 2pm 4pm 5pm 7pm

☐ Day ☐ Midday ☐ Evening

**Shops** Many shops in the resorts stay open throughout the day. Most shops are closed on Sundays.
**Banks** Banks are closed on Sundays.
**Restaurants** Many restaurants in the larger resorts are open daily from around 10am to midnight.
**Museums and attractions** Most museums are open Tuesday to Friday and Sunday 9:30–5:30.

**POLICE/FIRE/AMBULANCE 112**

## PERSONAL SAFETY

Crime is not a problem in Lanzarote. The greatest risk of theft is from another tourist. Put all belongings out of sight in the boot of your car when you are parked. If you are in self-catering accommodation lock all windows and doors before going out.

In an emergency call the police on 112 from any phone.

**Police assistance:**
☎ **112 from any phone**

## TELEPHONES

The cheapest way of making calls is to go to a *locutorio*. These can be found all over the island, in shopping centres or even as part of a local grocer's or souvenir shop. You are allocated a booth and then charged for the call afterwards. They are very cheap indeed, and a 20-minute call to mainland Europe in the evening costs little more than a couple of euros.

There are public telephones on most street corners with instructions in several languages. Most take coins or phonecards (*tarjetas telefónicas*), which are available from several outlets, though in practice they are not always stocked. The cheap rate for international calls is 10pm–8am and all day Sunday.

| International dialling codes Dial 00 followed by | |
| --- | --- |
| UK: | 44 |
| Ireland: | 353 |
| Germany: | 49 |
| USA: | 1 |

## POST

Postboxes are yellow and often have a slot marked *extranjeros* for mail abroad. Stamps (*sellos*) are available from post offices, hotels, news kiosks, tobacconists and some postcard shops.

A postcard to the UK or northern Europe will usually take about 7–10 days.

## ELECTRICITY

The power supply is 220 volts. Sockets take continental-style two-pin plugs. Visitors from the UK will require an adaptor, available at the airport and in the resorts.

## TIPS/GRATUITIES

Tipping is not expected for all services, and rates are lower than in some countries. As a general guide:

| | |
| --- | --- |
| Restaurants | 5–10% |
| Cafés/bars | Discretion |
| Tour guides | Discretion |
| Taxis | 10% |
| Hairdressers | 10% |
| Hotel staff | 10% |
| Lavatories | Discretion |

**UK**
☎ 928 262 508

**Ireland**
☎ 928 297 725

**Germany**
☎ 928 491 880

**Switzerland**
☎ 928 261 751

**Austria**
☎ 928 762 500

## HEALTH

**Insurance** Citizens of the European Union and certain other countries receive free medical treatment in Spain with the relevant documentation, although private medical insurance is still advised and is essential for all other visitors.

**Dental Services** Dental treatment has to be paid for by all visitors but is usually covered by private medical insurance.

**Weather** Visitors from cooler countries are especially vulnerable to the effects of the sun. You should cover up with a high-factor sunblock and drink plenty of non-alcoholic fluids. Children need to be well protected, especially when playing near the sea, as water and sand reflect the sun's rays.

**Drugs** Prescription and non-prescription drugs and medicines are available from pharmacies, usually distinguished by a large green cross. Outside normal hours, a notice on the door of each pharmacy should give the address of the nearest duty pharmacist.

**Safe Water** Tap water is generally safe to drink but has a high salt content. Mineral water is widely available and cheap, especially when bought at supermarkets in 5-litre (1.3-gallon) containers.

## CONCESSIONS

**Students** In general the Canary Islands do not attract backpacking youngsters and there are few if any youth or student concessions. There are no youth hostels and just two basic campsites, one at the Papagayo beaches and one on Isla la Graciosa.

**Senior Citizens** Lanzarote is an excellent destination for older travellers, especially in winter when the climate is clement. Some hotels and apartments offer long-stay discounts. The best deals are available through tour operators who specialise in holidays for senior citizens.

## TRAVELLING WITH A DISABILITY

All new buildings in Spain have to be equipped with wheelchair access, but many older hotels, apartment blocks and public buildings are still inaccessible. Some buses have doors that lower to ground level for wheelchair access. Before booking a holiday, you should discuss your particular needs with your tour operator or hotel.

## CHILDREN

Hotels and restaurants are generally very child-friendly, and many hotels have playgrounds, parks, mini-golf and children's pools. Some tour operators also provide children's clubs and activities as part of your holiday. However, facilities such as baby-changing rooms are rare.

## LAVATORIES

There are public lavatories in shopping centres and at some larger beaches. Other useful standbys are museums and bars.

## CUSTOMS

The import of wildlife souvenirs sourced from rare or endangered species may either be illegal or require a special permit. Before buying, check your home country's customs regulations.

# Useful Words and Phrases

es/no **Sí/no**
lease **Por favor**
hank you **Gracias**
ou're welcome **De nada**
lello **Hola**
ioodbye **Adiós**
iood morning **Buenos días**
iood afternoon **Buenas tardes**
iood night **Buenas noches**
low are you? **¿Qué tal?**
low much is this? **¿Cuánto vale?**
'm sorry **Lo siento**
xcuse me **Perdone**
'd like… **Me gustaría…**
)pen **Abierto**
:losed **Cerrado**

oday **Hoy**
omorrow **Mañana**
esterday **Ayer**
Monday **Lunes**
uesday **Martes**
Vednesday **Miércoles**
hursday **Jueves**
riday **Viernes**
iaturday **Sábado**
iunday **Domingo**

## IRECTIONS

'm lost **Me he perdido**
Vhere is…? **¿Dónde está…?**
low do I get to…?
  **¿Cómo se va…?**
  the bank **al banco**

the post office
  **a la oficina de correos**
Where are the lavatories?
  **¿Dónde están los servicios?**
Left **a la izquierda**
Right **a la derecha**
Straight on **todo recto**
At the traffic lights **en el semáforo**

## IF YOU NEED HELP

Help! **¡Socorro! / ¡Ayuda!**
Could you help me, please
  **¿Podría ayudarme, por favor?**
Do you speak English? **¿Habla inglés?**
I don't understand **No entiendo**
I don't speak Spanish
  **No hablo español**
Could you call a doctor?
  **¿Podría llamar a un médico,
  por favor?**

## ACCOMMODATION

Do you have a single/double room?
  **¿Le queda alguna habitación
  individual/doble?**
  with/without bath/WC/shower
  **con/sin baño propio/
  lavabo propio/ducha propia**
Does that include breakfast?
  **¿Incluye desayuno?**
I'll take this room
  **Me quedo con esta habitación**
The key to room…, please
  **La llave de la habitación…,
  por favor**

## UMBERS

| | | | | | | |
|---|---|---|---|---|---|---|
| | uno | 11 | once | 21 | veintiuno | 200 | doscientos |
| | dos | 12 | doce | 22 | veintidós | 300 | trescientos |
| | tres | 13 | trece | 30 | treinta | 400 | cuatrocientos |
| | cuatro | 14 | catorce | 40 | cuarenta | 500 | quinientos |
| | cinco | 15 | quince | 50 | cincuenta | 600 | seiscientos |
| | seis | 16 | dieciséis | 60 | sesenta | 700 | setecientos |
| | siete | 17 | diecisiete | 70 | setenta | 800 | ochocientos |
| | ocho | 18 | dieciocho | 80 | ochenta | 900 | novecientos |
| | nueve | 19 | diecinueve | 90 | noventa | 1000 | mil |
| 10 | diez | 20 | veinte | 100 | cien | | |

## RESTAURANT

I'd like to book a table
**Me gustaría reservar una mesa**
Have you got a table for two, please?
**¿Tienen una mesa para dos personas, por favor?**
Could we see the menu, please?
**¿Nos podría traer la carta, por favor?**
Could I have the bill, please?
**¿La cuenta, por favor?**
service charge included
**servicio incluido**

breakfast **el desayuno**
lunch **el almuerzo**
dinner **la cena**
table **una mesa**
waiter/waitress **camarero/camarera**
starters **los entremeses**
main course **los platos principales**
dessert **postres**
dish of the day **plato del día**
bill **la cuenta**

## MENU READER

**aceituna** olive
**ajo** garlic
**alcachofa** artichoke
**almejas** clams
**almendras** almonds
**anguila** eel
**arroz** rice
**atún/bonito** tuna

**bacalao** cod
**berenjena** aubergine (eggplant)
**biftec** steak
**bocadillo** sandwich
**boquerones** anchovies

**calamares** squid
**caldo** broth
**callos** tripe
**cangrejo** crab
**cebolla** onion
**cerdo** pork
**cerezas** cherries
**cerveza** beer
**champiñones** mushrooms
**chorizo** spicy sausage
**chuleta** chop
**churros** fritters
**ciruela** plum
**cochinillo asado** roast suckling pig
**codorniz** quail
**conejo** rabbit
**cordero** lamb

**crema** cream
**criadillas** sweetbreads
**crudo** raw

**endibia** chicory
**ensalada (mixta)** mixed salad
**ensaladilla rusa** Russian salad
**espárragos** asparagus
**espinaca** spinach

**fideos** noodles
**filete** fillet
**flan** crème caramel
**frambuesa** raspberry
**fresa** strawberry
**fruta (de temporada)** seasonal fruit

**galleta** biscuit (cookie)
**gambas** prawns
**garbanzos** chickpeas
**gazpacho andaluz** gazpacho (cold soup)
**grosellas** red/black currants
**guisantes** peas

**habas** broad beans
**helado** ice cream
**hígado de oca** goose liver

**huevos fritos/ revueltos** fried/scrambled eggs

**jamón** ham
**judías verdes** French beans
**jugo** fruit juice

**langosta** lobster
**langostino** crayfish
**leche** milk
**lechuga** lettuce
**legumbres** vegetables
**lengua** tongue
**lenguado** sole
**liebre** hare
**lomo de cerdo** pork tenderloin

**manzana** apple
**mariscos** seafood
**mejillones** mussels
**melocotón** peach
**melón** melon
**merluza** hake
**mero** sea bass
**morcilla** black pudding

**pan** bread
**pato** duck
**pepinillos** gherkins
**pepino** cucumber
**pera** pear

**perdiz** partridge
**perejil** parsley
**pescado** fish
**pez espada** swordfish
**pimientos** red/ green peppers
**piña** pineapple
**plátano** banana
**pollo** chicken
**puerro** leek
**pulpo** octopus

**queso** cheese

**rape** monkfish
**riñones** kidneys
**rodaballo** turbot

**salchicha** sausag
**salchichón** salam
**salmón** salmon
**salmonete** red mullet
**solomillo de buey** fillet of beef
**sopa** soup

**tocino** bacon
**tortilla española** Spanish omelette
**tortilla francesa** plain omelette
**trucha** trout

**verduras** green vegetables

**zanahorias** carrot

# Atlas

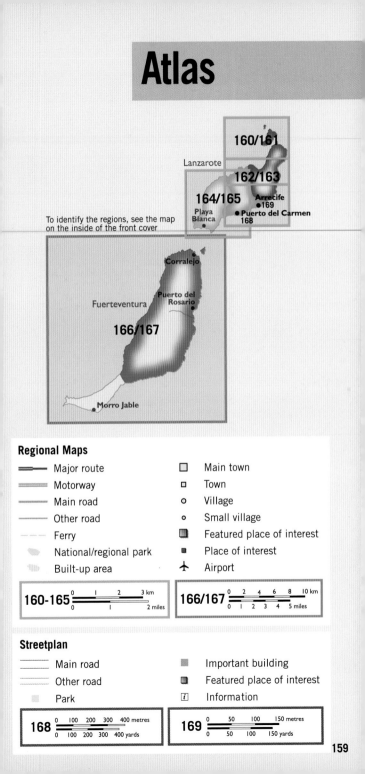

160/161

Lanzarote

162/163

164/165

Arrecife
●169
●Puerto del Carmen
168

Playa
Blanca

To identify the regions, see the map
on the inside of the front cover

Corralejo

Puerto del
Rosario

Fuerteventura

166/167

Morro Jable

## Regional Maps

| ═══ | Major route | ☐ | Main town |
| ═══ | Motorway | ◻ | Town |
| ▬▬ | Main road | ○ | Village |
| ── | Other road | ○ | Small village |
| - - - | Ferry | ▣ | Featured place of interest |
|  | National/regional park | ■ | Place of interest |
|  | Built-up area | ✈ | Airport |

**160-165** | 0  1  2  3 km / 0  1  2 miles

**166/167** | 0  2  4  6  8  10 km / 0  1  2  3  4  5 miles

## Streetplan

| ═══ | Main road |  | Important building |
| ▬▬ | Other road | ▣ | Featured place of interest |
|  | Park | 𝑖 | Information |

**168** | 0  100  200  300  400 metres / 0  100  200  300  400 yards

**169** | 0  50  100  150 metres / 0  50  100  150 yards

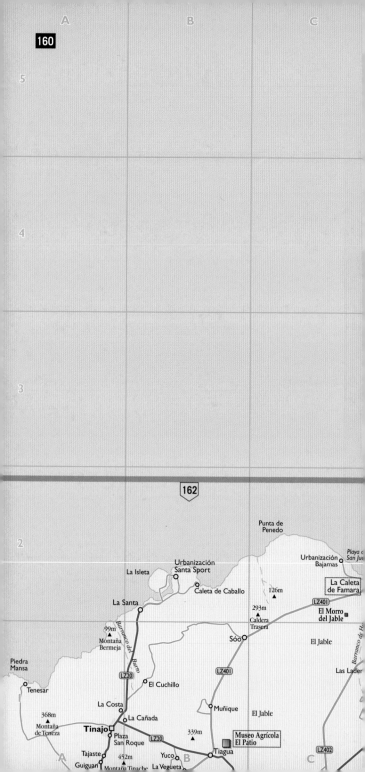

162

Punta de
Penedo

Urbanización
Santa Sport

La Isleta

Caleta de Caballo

126m

293m
Caldera
Trasera

Urbanización
Bajamas

Playa c
San Jua

La Caleta
de Famara

LZ401

El Morro
del Jable

La Santa

99m
Montaña
Bermeja

Sóo

El Jable

Barranco de Ho

Piedra
Mansa

Tenesar

LZ20

El Cuchillo

LZ401

Las Lader

La Costa

La Cañada

Muñique

El Jable

368m
Montaña
de Teneza

Tinajo

Plaza
San Roque

LZ20

339m

Museo Agrícola
El Patio

Tajaste

452m

Yuco

Tiagua

LZ402

Guiguan

Montaña Tinache

La Vegueta

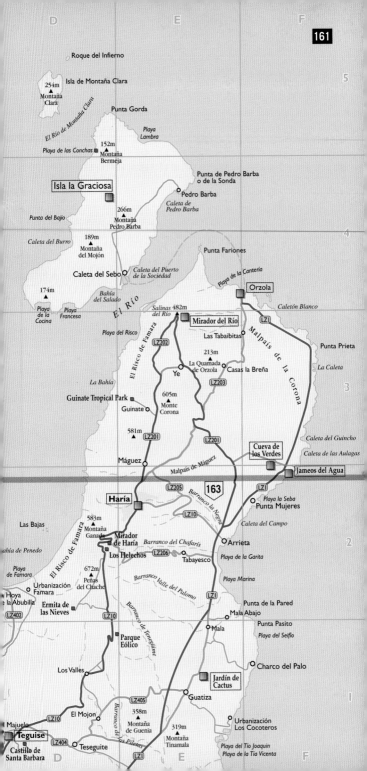

Roque del Infierno

Isla de Montaña Clara

254m
▲
Montaña
Clara

Punta Gorda

*El Río de Montaña Clara*

*Playa
Lambra*

152m
▲
Montaña
Bermeja

*Playa de las Conchas*

Punta de Pedro Barba
o de la Sonda

Pedro Barba

*Caleta de
Pedro Barba*

**Isla la Graciosa**

*Punta del Bajio*

266m
▲
Montaña
Pedro Barba

*Caleta del Burro*

189m
▲
Montaña
del Mojón

Punta Fariones

*Caleta del Puerto
de la Sociedad*

Caleta del Sebo

*Playa de la Cantería*

174m
▲

*Bahía
del Salado*

**Orzola**

*Caletón Blanco*

*Playa
de la
Cocina*

*Playa
Francesa*

*El Río*

LZ1

Punta Prieta

Salinas
del Río

482m
▲

**Mirador del Río**

Las Tabaibitas

*Malpaís de la Corona*

*La Caleta*

*Playa del Risco*

LZ202

213m
▲
La Quamada
de Orzola

Casas la Breña

*El Risco de Famara*

Ye

LZ203

*La Bahía*

**Guinate Tropical Park**

605m
▲
Monte
Corona

Guinate

*Caleta del Guincho*

581m
▲

LZ201

*Caleta de las Aulagas*

LZ201

**Cueva de
los Verdes**

Máguez

*Malpaís de Máguez*

**Jameos del Agua**

LZ1

LZ205

**163**

LZ1

**Haría**

*Barranco de la Negra*

*Playa la Seba*
Punta Mujeres

Las Bajas

583m
▲
Montaña
Ganada

LZ10

*Caleta del Campo*

*Bahía de Penedo*

Mirador
de Haría

*Barranco del Chafarís*

**Arrieta**

Los Helechos

LZ206

Tabayesco

*Playa de la Garita*

*Playa
de Famara*

672m
▲
Peñas
del Chache

*El Risco de Famara*

*Barranco Valle del Palomo*

*Playa Marina*

a Hoya
de la Abubilla

*Barranco de Tenegüime*

LZ1

Punta de la Pared

Urbanización
de Famara

**Ermita de
las Nieves**

Mala Abajo

LZ402

LZ10

Mala

Punta Pasito

*Playa del Seifío*

Parque
Eólico

Charco del Palo

Los Valles

**Jardín de
Cactus**

Majuela

LZ405

Guatiza

LZ10

El Mojón

358m
▲
Montaña
de Guenia

Urbanización
Los Cocoteros

**Teguise**

LZ404

*Barranco de los Pileteros*

319m
▲
Montaña
Tinamala

*Playa del Tío Joaquín
Playa de la Tía Vicenta*

Castillo de
Santa Barbara

Teseguite

LZ1

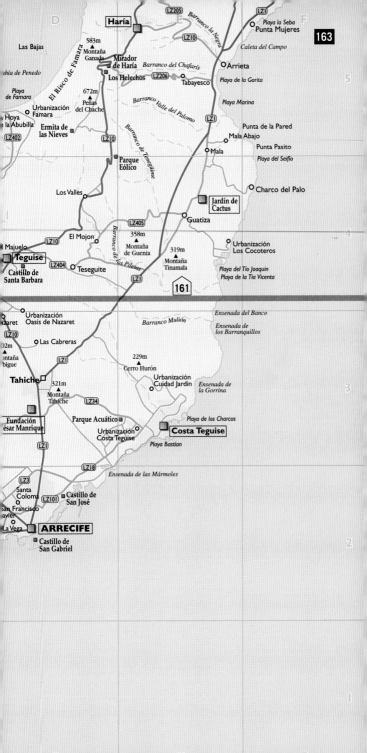

**Haría**

LZ205

LZ1

Playa la Seba
Punta Mujeres

Caleta del Campo

Las Bajas

583m
Montaña
Ganada

LZ10

Barranco la Negra

Arrieta

Mirador
de Haría

Barranco del Chafarís

Playa de la Garita

Los Helechos

LZ206

Tabayesco

El Risco de Famara

672m
Peñas
del Chache

Playa Marina

ahía de Penedo

Playa
de Famara

Barranco Valle del Palomo

Punta de la Pared

Mala Abajo

Urbanización
Famara

a Hoya
la Abubilla

LZ10

LZ1

Mala

Punta Pasito

Ermita de
las Nieves

Playa del Seifio

LZ402

Barranco de Tenegüime

Parque
Eólico

Charco del Palo

Los Valles

Jardín de
Cactus

Barranco de los Pileta

LZ405

Guatiza

Majuelo

El Mojón

358m
Montaña
de Guenia

319m
Montaña
Tinamala

Urbanización
Los Cocoteros

LZ10

**Teguise**

LZ404

Teseguite

LZ1

Playa del Tío Joaquin
Playa de la Tía Vicenta

Castillo de
Santa Barbara

**161**

Ensenada del Banco

Urbanización
Oasis de Nazaret

Barranco Mulión

Ensenada de
los Barranquillos

azaret

LZ10

02m
ontaña
bigue

Las Cabreras

LZ1

229m
Cerro Hurón

**Tahiche**

321m
Montaña
Tahiche

Urbanización
Cuidad Jardin

Ensenada de
la Gorrina

LZ34

Parque Acuático

Playa de los Charcos

Fundación
ésar Manrique

Urbanización
Costa Teguise

**Costa Teguise**

LZ1

Playa Bastian

LZ18

Ensenada de las Mármoles

LZ3

Santa
Coloma

LZ101

Castillo de
San José

an Francisco
avier

La Vega

**ARRECIFE**

Castillo de
San Gabriel

D

E

F

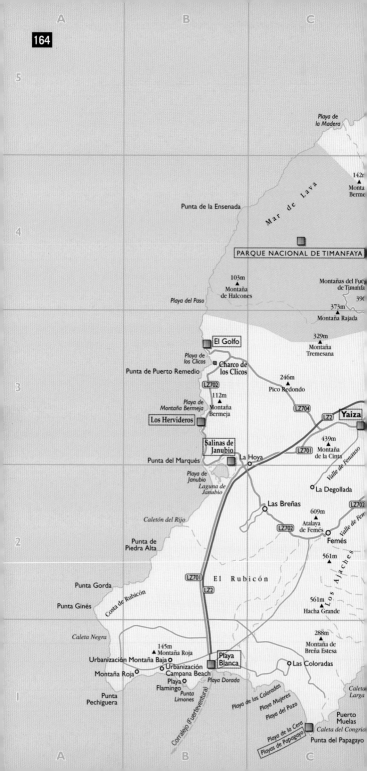

Playa de
la Madera

142m
Monta
Berme

Punta de la Ensenada

M a r   d e   L a v a

PARQUE NACIONAL DE TIMANFAYA

103m
Montaña
de Halcones

Montañas del Fue
de Timanfa

390

Playa del Paso

373m
Montaña Rajada

329m
Montaña
Tremesana

El Golfo

Playa de
los Clicos

Charco de
los Clicos

Punta de Puerto Remedio

246m
Pico Redondo

LZ702

112m
Montaña
Bermeja

Playa de
Montaña Bermeja

LZ704

LZ7

Yaiza

Los Hervideros

439m
Montaña
de la Cinta

Salinas de
Janubio

LZ701

Punta del Marqués

La Hoya

Valle de Fenauso

Playa de
Janubio

Laguna de
Janubio

La Degollada

Las Breñas

LZ702

Caletón del Rijo

609m
Atalaya
de Femés

LZ702

Valle de Fem

Punta de
Piedra Alta

Femés

561m

Punta Gorda

LZ701

El   R u b i c ó n

Punta Ginés

LZ2

Costa de Rubicón

561m
Hacha Grande

L o s   A j a c h e s

Caleta Negra

145m
Montaña Roja

288m
Montaña de
Breña Estesa

Urbanización Montaña Baja

Playa
Blanca

Las Coloradas

Montaña Roja

Urbanización
Campana Beach

Caleta
Larga

Playa
Flamingo

Playa Dorada

Punta
Pechiguera

Punta
Limones

Corralejo (Fuerteventura)

Playa de las Coloradas

Playa Mujeres

Playa del Pozo

Puerto
Muelas

Playa de la Cera

Caleta del Congrio

Playas de Papagayo

Punta del Papagayo

A          B          C

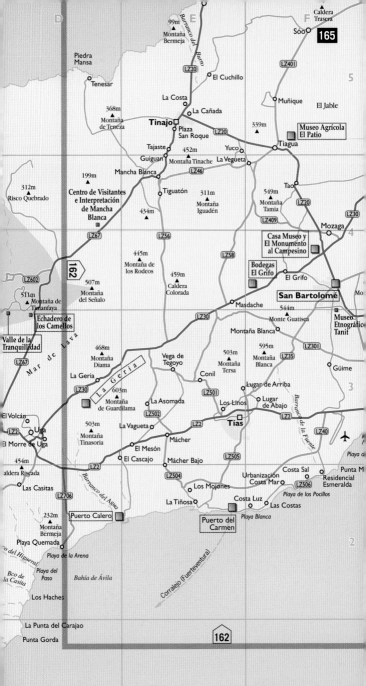

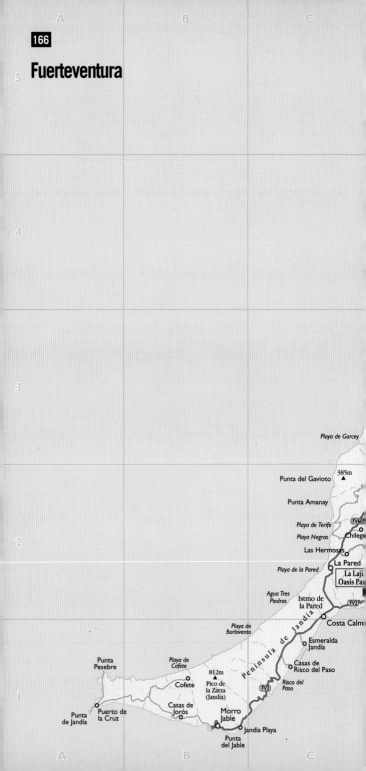

# Fuerteventura

*Playa de Garcey*

Punta del Gavioto    385m ▲

Punta Amanay

*Playa de Terife*    FV60
*Playa Negras*    Chilegu

Las Hermosas

*Playa de la Pared*    La Pared
La Laji
Oasis Pa

*Agua Tres
Piedras*    Istmo de
la Pared    FV2

Costa Calm

*Playa de
Barlovento*    Esmeralda
Jandía

Punta
Pesebre    *Playa de
Cofete*    Casas de
Risco del Paso

Cofete    812m ▲
Pico de
la Zarza
(Jandía)    *Risco del
Paso*    FV2

Casas de
Jorós

Punta
de Jandía    Puerto de
la Cruz    Morro
Jable

Jandía Playa

Punta
del Jable

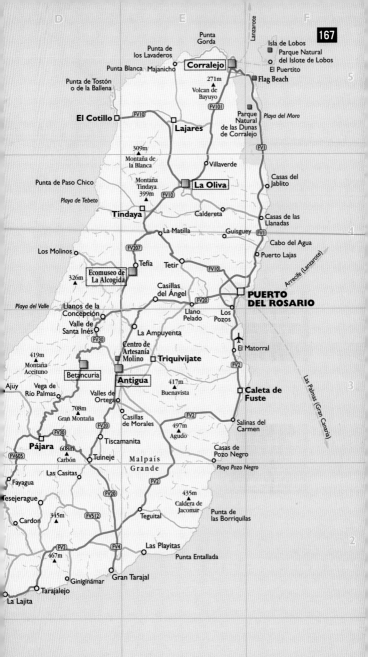

Punta
Gorda

Punta de
los Lavaderos

Isla de Lobos

Parque Natural
del Islote de Lobos

Punta Blanca   Majanicho        **Corralejo**        El Puertito

Punta de Tostón                                      Flag Beach
o de la Ballena                271m

Volcán de
Bayuyo

FV101

**El Cotillo** □   FV10                              Parque      Playa del Moro
                    **Lajares**        Natural
                                       de las Dunas
                                       de Corralejo    FV1

309m
Montaña de
la Blanca                          Villaverde

Montaña                                             Casas del
Tindaya                                             Jablito
Punta de Paso Chico   399m         **La Oliva** □
                      ▲

Playa de Tebeto                                     Casas de las
                                                    Llanadas

                    **Tindaya** □        Caldereta     FV1

                                                    Guisguey   Cabo del Agua

Los Molinos ○       La Matilla                       Puerto Lajas

                    FV207
                                                              Arrecife (Lanzarote)
Ecomuseo de        Tefia    Tetir      FV10
**La Alcogida**

326m ▲                      Casillas
                            del Ángel

Playa del Valle                    FV20        **PUERTO
                                                DEL ROSARIO**
Llanos de la
Concepción                  Llano      Los
                            Pelado    Pozos
Valle de
Santa Inés         La Ampuyenta

                   Centro de           ✈ El Matorral
419m               Artesanía
Montaña            Molino   **Triquivijate**    FV2
Aceituno

**Betancuria** ▢                       417m
                   **Antigua** □       Buenavista     □ **Caleta de
                                                         Fuste**
Ajuy ◖             Vega de   Valles de
                   Río Palmas  Ortega
                                       FV2
           708m             Casillas
           Gran Montaña     de Morales    Salinas del
                    FV20                  Carmen
                   497m
**Pájara** □       Tiscamanita  Agudo
           608m                        Casas de
FV605      Carbón   Tuineje           Pozo Negro
                            M a l p a í s   Playa Pozo Negro
Las Casitas        G r a n d e
                            FV2
Fayagua ○

Tesejerague ○                          435m
                   FV512               Caldera de
Cardón ○   345m                        Jacomar   Punta de
           ▲                                      las Borriquilas
                   Teguital
           FV2     FV4
467m                        Las Playitas
▲                                     Punta Entallada
           Giniginámar   Gran Tarajal
Tarajalejo

La Lajita

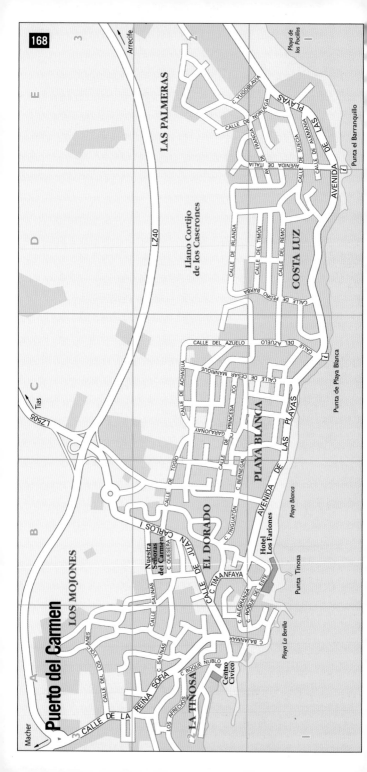

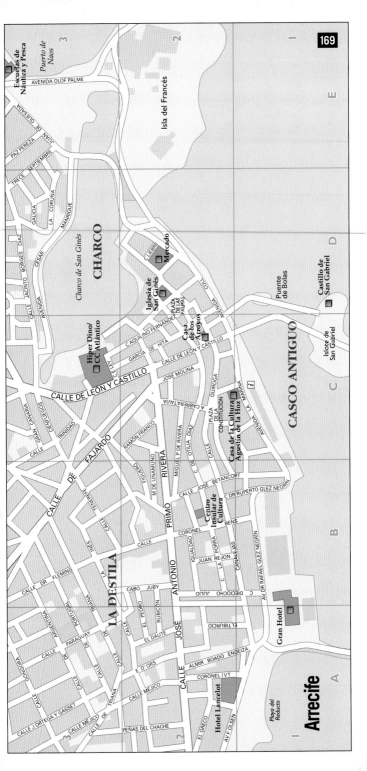

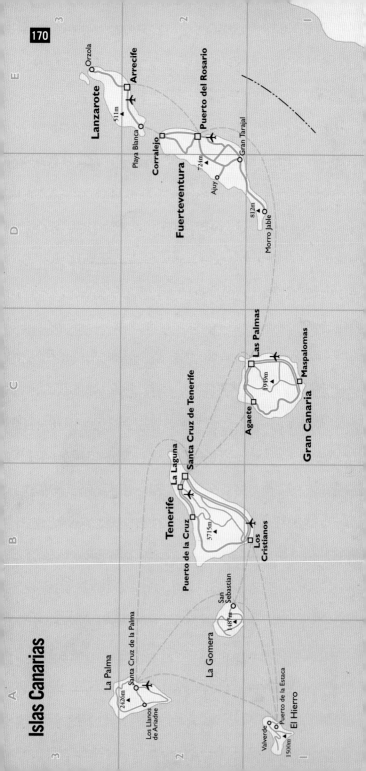

# Islas Canarias

**170**

La Palma
2426m
Los Llanos de Aridane
Santa Cruz de la Palma

La Gomera
1487m
San Sebastián

El Hierro
1500m
Valverde
Puerto de la Estaca

**Tenerife**
3715m
Puerto de la Cruz
La Laguna
**Santa Cruz de Tenerife**
Los Cristianos

**Gran Canaria**
1949m
Agaete
**Las Palmas**
Maspalomas

**Fuerteventura**
724m
Corralejo
**Puerto del Rosario**
Gran Tarajal
Ajuy
812m
Morro Jable

**Lanzarote**
511m
Orzola
**Arrecife**
Playa Blanca